Post Globalisation Politics of Language in Maharashtra

Post Globalisation Politics of Language in Maharashtra

DOCTOR OF PHILOSOPHY

In Politics

DEEPAK TANAJI PAWAR

GYAN

The Publication of this thesis was financially upheld by ICSSR and the responsibility of the facts stated, opinions expressed or conclusions reached are entirely that of the author and ICSSR accepts no responsibility for them.

ICSSR Consultant

Professor Sanjay Lodha, Evaluator of this Thesis.

ISBN : 978-81-212-1320-2

Price : ₹ 498

First Published, 2016

Published by

Gyan Publishing House
5, Ansari Road
Daryaganj, New Delhi-110002
Phones: 9811692060
E-mail: books@gyanbooks.com

Printed at: G. Print Process, Delhi.

Cataloging in Publication Data—DK
Courtesy: D.K. Agencies (P) Ltd. <docinfo@dkagencies.com>

Pawar, Deepak Tanaji, author.
Post globalisation politics of language in Maharashtra : synopsis of the thesis to be submitted for the degree of Doctor of Philosophy in politics / Mr. Deepak Tanaji Pawar.
pages cm
Includes bibliographical references.
ISBN 9788121213202

1. Marathi language—Government policy—India—Maharashtra. 2. Language policy—India—Maharashtra. 3. Maharashtra (India)—Politics and government—20th century. I. Title.

P119.32.I4P39 2016 DDC 306.4495479 23

Dedication

I want to dedicate this book to my wife Sandhya and daughter Shravani

Contents

Preface

Writing about language policy and language politics in our turbulent times is not without consequences. It is easily labeled as parochial, sectarian and contributing to the disintegration of the country. I think otherwise. I look at the understanding of language policy and language politics in India as a tool to decode the complex reality and provide practical solutions to the perplexing situations of our times.

I ventured into the study of Language Policy and politics in Maharashtra primarily as an activist. However at a later stage I realized that I need to put my understanding in a framework and be ready for uncomfortable questions. These uncomfortable questions and my attempt to answer them form a major part of this book. During the period that I spent for my Ph.D. I kept raising these questions which occasionally the activist in me was highly angry about. But through a series of discussions with my guide and reading of material hitherto undiscovered, made me pitch deeper and take my intellectual understanding and activism to the next level.

Post globalisation politics of Language in Maharashtra is an attempt to understand the changing rationale of language policy and politics in India using Maharashtra as the reference point. So the conclusions drawn from Maharashtra can have a Pan-Indian appeal. To put it the other way round, unless we strive hard to have an all India language policy and corroborating institutional and financial setup, it is not possible to have state-wise success. Therefore I look at this entire research as a pilot project. More would follow from me and also many others from the academic and activist fraternity.

The takeaways from this whole process could be the desire to read more, to interact with people with contrary views and overall be more patient about the process and success of language activism. I take this opportunity to thank my guide Dr Uttara Sahasrabuddhe, for engaging in a serious dialogue where we differed on many occasions. I would also like to thank various members of the academic and activist fraternity who spared their time for discussions with me. I thank Dr. Vaidehi Daptardar and Dr. Sudha Vyas, principals of my college for granting me two years of leave under faculty improvement program. I thank the University Grant Commission for the leave. Last but not the least I thank my wife Sandhya and daughter Shravani for bearing with me during this time.

Deepak Pawar

Acknowledgements

It gives me a sense of satisfaction to have completed this thesis. In a span of more than five years that I am associated with this topic my understanding of the topic has undergone major changes. The whole exercise of reading, writing and interacting with people during this period has been quite enriching. It has given me an opportunity to look at the subject matter from multiple angles and revisit my own ideological predispositions. At the end of this exercise, I have many more questions in mind. I hope some of them will be answered in due course.

I began this exercise as the extension of the language activism that I am involved in. It is my guide Dr Uttara Sahasrabuddhe who brought me out of that comfort zone and raised certain questions which I have tried to answer through the Thesis. Being a liberal at heart, she gave me the freedom to express my ideas and ensured that I stick to the methodology. Eventually, the whole exercise became quite collaborative. I thank her for her patience and the dialogue which has helped me improve my thinking.

I thank the UGC for granting me two years leave under the Faculty Improvement Programme. It gave me the time required for concentrating on the research. I thank present and former principals of my college (Dr Sudha Vyas and Dr Vaidehi Daptardar) for granting the leave. I thank Dr Surendra Jondhale, Head Department of Civics and Politics for his co-operation at every stage.

I had the opportunity to interact with Dr Aruna Pendse, Dr Suhas Palshikar, and Professor Ram Bapat. Their insightful suggestions have helped me in improving the thesis. I also had the opportunity to interact with MNS president Raj Thackeray, Secretary of the Yashwantrao Chavan Pratishthan. Mr Sharad Kale and members of various organisations working for Marathi. Interaction with my colleagues at Marathi Abhyas Kendra, especially Dr Prakash Parab has been quite enriching. I thank the respondents of various questionnaires for their prompt response.

I have referred books from many libraries for the Thesis. I thank the staff of J.N. Library, Kalina, University of Mumbai K.J. Somaiya College of Arts and Commerce Library, Department of Civics and Politics Library, Yashwantrao Chavan Pratishthan's Library for their cooperation. I thank my students Anushree Gavas and Rohini Nayar for their assistance. I would also like to thank Dr Datta Pawar and Dr D.N. Dhanagare for making available some rare books needed for the thesis. I thank my friend Dr Vaibhavi Palsule for her encouragement and help in all administrative matters.

Throughout these two years, my wife Sandhya has been very supportive and handled my mood swings quite patiently. Without her help, things would not have been as smooth as they have been. My daughter Shravani kept on enquiring about the completion of thesis so that she can use the computer for playing games. Both of them have given me the emotional strength that I needed in this period. To thank them would be too formal. Lastly, I wish to thank all my friends and members of the family who encouraged me during the research.

Converting a thesis into a book is a tough task. My students Aasawari Phadke, Sharvari Agashe, Vikrant Pande and Abhijit Auchar gave me valuable inputs to make the work more interesting. Due to paucity of time, I could not undertake major changes. I thank them for their help.

I thank ICSSR for the financial support and Professor Sanjay Lodha for evaluating the thesis on behalf of ICSSR. I thank the Gyan Publishing House team for their patience.

Dr Deepak Pawar

6, Agrawal Bhavan,
Asalpha Village, Ghatkopar West
Mumbai 400084
deepak.pawar@civics.mu.ac.in

09820437665

Chapter 1

Introduction

Language politics as identity based politics has been a subject of major political concern in independent India. Language has played a major role in the reorganisation of the country through administrative and linguistic convenience. After the country had been linguistically reorganised, doubts were raised about its impact on the unity and integrity of the country. The problems in Assam, Tamil Nadu, and Punjab were partially linked with the issues of language and linguistic consciousness. Thus, real or perceived injustice to a linguistic community has been a major concern after independence. Similarly, the ways and means of making the use of official languages of the states in various domains of social life has also been a matter of intense debate. The failure of state governments in delivering the results in this regard has contributed to the emergence of civil society movements for the preservation of various languages and cultures across the country. With the onslaught of globalisation, especially cultural globalisation- of which English language works as the vehicle, linguistic identities are facing a severe challenge of survival. Thus, the issue of language and culture preservation and empowerment of linguistic identities has become more complicated than before. It is against this backdrop that I intend to study this subject.

Language and language politics have also been a matter of academic scrutiny although exclusive studies on all-India patterns of language politics are limited in number.[1] Before venturing into the topic of present research, it would be worthwhile taking a review of some of the literature on the subject.

1.1 Review of Literature

Some of the studies of language politics that we are going to review are not exclusively focused on it. They deal with identity politics and within that ambit look at language politics. Some are pan-Indian in approach. There are theoretical debates about the evolving nature of identity politics and its interface with the forces of globalisation. Together they give us an insight into the nature of language politics in India in general and Maharashtra in particular. Then there are studies dealing with the Samyukta Maharashtra movement and Shivsena. Some of them are done by participants, whereas others by distant observers.

Lalji Pendse's diary of the Samyukta Maharashtra movement[2] deals with the dynamics of the movement. The book is not merely a diary of events. It deals with the history of Marathi and Maharashtra and then goes on to explain the series of events in the struggle. The author being a participant in the movement is passionate about the movement. He gives an insider's account of the movement that got dismantled after achieving its primary goal of creation of Unified Maharashtra. The book is important in more than one sense that it brings to the fore the discourse of the Samyukta Maharashtra Movement and helps us in understanding how it underwent changes in later years.

Dr Y.D. Phadke's thesis on the Samyukta Maharashtra Movement[3] deals with politics of language in the aftermath of independence. It gives an elaborate analysis of the 'Samyukta Maharashtra Movement' against the backdrop of countrywide demands for linguistic reorganisation of states. It provides inputs about processes that unified Maharashtra and talks about the 'unfinished agenda' of inclusion of border areas like Belgaum and Nipani into unified Maharashtra. The focus of the book being the study of the 'Samyukta Maharashtra Movement', it naturally doesn't mull too much over the post-1960 developments. In the later stage of his academic career, Dr Phadke wrote an eight volume history of Maharashtra.[4] Volumes 6-8 of this work focus on the genesis and development of 'Samyukta Maharashtra Movement'. The prefaces that Dr Phadke wrote for these volumes give an insight into his ideas of ethnic movements. This is a monumental work in the sense that it gives huge resources for a researcher or an activist to compare and contrast the 'Samyukta Maharashtra Movement' with later political agencies like Shivsena and Maharashtra Navnirman Sena.

Mary Fainsod Katzenstein's Ethnicity and Equality: The Shiv Sena Party and Preferential Policies in Bombay[5] deals with the emergence of Shivsena against the backdrop of creation of unified Maharashtra. She focuses on the way in which Shivsena mobilised urban middle class Maharashtrian youth against outsiders (South Indians in general and Keralites in particular) who were perceived to be usurping the jobs that the sons-of-the soil expected should go to them. She deals with the techniques of mobilisation, the migration scenario and the response of the state that culminated into preferential policies. One of the major issues that she debates is about the definition of Marathi that Shivsena espoused. The idea that whoever speaks Marathi language should be given preference was eventually diluted to provide for the principle of domicile. This meant that anybody who has stayed in this state for a period of 15 years[6] would be called Maharashtrian irrespective of his or her mother tongue. This has repercussions for later developments in language politics in Maharashtra.

Dipankar Gupta's book on Shivsena[7] deals with the roots of nativism and its impact on the politics of the state of Maharashtra. He rightly points out that the state Congress and the capitalist forces have successfully used Shivsena to counter the threat of socialists and communists especially in the field of trade unions. He discusses Shivsena's use of violence as a strategy and its use in the long run. His prediction based on Gramsci's idea of integral autonomy of subaltern classes that the final dissolution of the attraction of Nativist and regional ideologies can be accomplished by energetic left wing praxis (p.199) has however not come true.

Ironically, both these books do not discuss the roots of the Shivsena in the Samyukta Maharashtra Movement and the hopes that it created.[8] This is discussed at length in the chapter on Shivsena.

The book by Amruta Basu and Atul Kohli (Ed.), *Community Conflicts and the State in India* – (1998, OUP)[9] deals with the interface between conflict and regional / linguistic identities. In a way, it focuses on the crisis of governability intensified by identity politics. In one of the articles written by Mary Fainsod Katzenstein, Uday Singh Mehta and Usha Thakkar titled 'The Rebirth of Shivsena in Maharashtra: The Symbiosis of Discursive and Institutional Power' the authors review Shivsena's conscious shift from the ideology of Sons-of-soil to Hindutva. It analyses contesting viewpoints about Shivsena's departure from nativist politics and causes thereof. It also focuses on the methods used by Shivsena to try and ensure the co-existence of the nativist and Hindutva agenda. However, it doesn't tell much about the damage this has caused to the politics of language. Nor does it suggest how a different form of Nativist politics could have evolved had Shivsena stuck to its Nativist agenda. In a way it is more of a commentary about the ills of communal politics adopted by Shivsena post-1985.

In addition to the books written by academicians, there are some written by journalists/ media persons. Vaibhav Purandare's *Sena Story*[10] is a journalistic account of the growth of Shivsena. He deals with Shivsena's shift from the Marathi Manoos agenda to Hindutva and its performance in power. A firsthand account of Shivsena leadership derived through interviews is a strength of this book. However, it does not analyze governance issues that a mobilisation like Shivsena creates. The impressionistic nature of the account in this book makes it less useful for further studies.

Prakash Akolkar's Marathi book on Shivsena[11] is more critical in nature and gives a detailed account of intra party politics within Shivsena and its drifting away from the Marathi agenda.

It gives a detailed description of the pioneering work done by 'Sthaniya Lokadhikar Samiti' (Committee for the protection of the rights of locals) established by Shivsena in the early phase of its career and how this work was eventually ignored when Shivsena shifted to Hindutva in search of power. However, this book doesn't aim at condemnation of Shivsena.

"Maharashtratil Sattantar"[12] by Rajendra Vora and Suhas Palshikar deals with the debacle of the Congress and the rise of Shivsena-BJP alliance on the backdrop of 1995 Vidhan Sabha elections in Maharashtra through constituency and region-wise electoral statistics. It tries to establish the relationship between urbanisation, new economic policy and ascendancy of neo-fascist forces like Shivsena - BJP. Indirectly, it establishes the success rate of language politics in Maharashtra. However, globalisation, being an emerging phenomenon then, the book doesn't elaborate on the relevance of the linguistic agenda in the changed atmosphere.

In his edited volume '*Maharashtratil Sattasangharsha*' (power struggle in Maharashtra) Dr Suhas Palshikar[13] and his team has given a statistical analysis of the performance of major political parties in Maharashtra. In his account of Shivsena, Palshikar asks a few questions about the organisational structure of the Shivsena and its changing caste base. He deals with Shivsena's ideological discourse based on the appeal to masculinity as its core component suggesting that violence, use of muscle power and encouraging resistance has been integral to the functioning of Shivsena. This, he argues, has attracted people, especially the youth in metropolitan areas. Palshikar argues that Shivsena's politics is based on the opposition to the 'Other'. It is a product of the inferiority complex of the people who are principal supporters of the movement. He bases his criticism on the dictatorial and fascist nature of Shivsena's leadership. He does not see much benefit in Shivsena's exclusionist brand of politics. However, he does not suggest an alternate brand of language politics as far as Maharashtra is concerned.

Thomas Blom Hansen's *Urban violence in India: Identity politics, Mumbai and the postcolonial city*[14] deals with the violence in the city of Mumbai especially the 1992-1993 riots and its impact on the identity of the city. In a way, it deals with 'Vernacularisation of democracy' in the country with special focus on the city. The challenges put forth by militant conflicts like Shivsena pose challenges to the very notion of rule of law, he contends. It is however, important to trace the process of ascending legitimisation of linguistic communities as beneficiaries in the context of 'identity politics', which is not done by the author very comprehensively.

For quite some time, there was no material made available by Shivsena. However, this gap has been filled by two recent ventures by one of its seniormost leaders Manohar Joshi. He wrote a thick volume titled '*Shivsena – Kaal, Aaj, and Udya*' (Shivsena- yesterday, today and tomorrow).[15] It gives detailed information about the evolution of Shivsena from a small organisation of rebellious youth to a major party in Maharashtra. Mr Joshi has provided material from Shivsena's mouthpieces Marmik and Saamna which gives us an opportunity to understand the dynamics of politics. However, as the author has himself explained, it is mere documentation and not a commentary on Shivsena. A number of issues related to Marathi language and Marathi Manoos that Shivsena took up in its early phase have not been resolved or resurfaced. Mr Joshi should have discussed this. But he has resisted himself from doing so probably because he is still active in Shivsena.

His thesis[16] is even more silent on this issue. He deals with the role of Shivsena as a regional party and analyses its success and failure. While doing that however he does not focus on the limitations of the Shivsena ideology and its effect on identity politics in Maharashtra. Thus, the thesis is a mere summary of events that the Shivsena has gone through with a brief comparison of other regional political parties. Unfortunately, the thesis neither provides a credible defense of Shivsena, nor does it chart out details of its future course of action.

Having discussed the writings specific to Maharashtra we can now move on to works with a broader analysis having a pan-Indian approach in mind.

Jyotirindra Das Gupta's *Language Conflict and National Development: Group Politics and National language policy in India.* (1970, University of California Press)[17] details the interface between the nationalist movement and linguistic movements and its impact on the making of Indian Federation. It deals extensively with the official language problem and its impact on inter-state as well as centre-state relations. However, problems of marginalisation of official languages and the consequent struggle for protection and preservation of linguistic identity in the wake of cultural homogenisation facilitated by Globalisation do not get any mention in the book. The reason is obvious. These forces hardly existed or mattered when the book was written.

Robert D King's *Nehru and the Language Politics of India* (1997, OUP)[18] is a holistic attempt to understand Nehru's mind in dealing with issues of linguistic reorganisation. As a historical linguist, King argues that the state can't really do much in establishing language priorities. He says that Nehru's recalcitrant approach in dealing with linguistic demands actually helped him in minimising linguistic violence. However, in contemporary times when the State is withdrawing to accommodate the market and transnational forces, we need to ask whether such a distant approach in handling language issues could lead to legitimisation of cultural monism thereby making identity politics look either uncivil or redundant.

Bipin Chandra, Mridula Mukherjee and Aditya Mukherjee's edited volume '*India after independence 1947-2000*' (2000, Penguin books)[19] provides chronological developments after independence. It deals with linguistic reorganisation of states, growth of regionalism and politics of regional inequalities. It is not a critique of linguistic movements or politics, but provides details about the issues involved in identity formation in post-independence India.

It works as a background note for the analysis of politics of language. Sudipta Kaviraj's edited volume 'Politics in India (Oxford in India: Readings in sociology and social anthropology)' (1997, OUP) deals with issues of social structure, caste, class. It has a special section on sociology of identity wherein Dipankar Gupta deals with the interface of nation-state and language politics. He provides a comparison of AASU (All Assam Students' Union), Shivsena and others nativist outfits. Ethnicising of politics and its impact on the idea of the federation are part of the discussions in the book. However, it is primarily a review of the past and does not emphasise the impact of post-globalisation forces on language politics.

Problems of identity politics based on language that India has encountered are not unique to India. Neighbouring South Asian countries like Sri Lanka and Pakistan have faced similar problems. Tariq Rahman has analysed the language and politics interface in Pakistan in detail.[20] He has discussed the conflict between Urdu and other provincial languages in Pakistan for survival and supremacy. He also directs our attention to the role of the political elite in use or non-use of a language thus raising the crucial point that language development or promotion is a part of the political process. One major difference that we see between India and Pakistan is the absence of linguistic reorganisation in Pakistan that has complicated linguistic issues even further. Similarly, Partha Ghosh's account of ethnic politics in Sri Lanka[21] discusses the Tamil versus Sinhala controversy in Sri Lanka that led to the demands of secession. One of the major impediments in the resolution of this conflict was the reorganisation of states and consequent devolution of power. This comparison gives us an understanding that however troublesome the linguistic reorganisation of states in India might have been, it was a blessing in disguise in the sense that it diffused future tension between linguistic communities.

On this backdrop we can move on to the issues of identity politics created by globalisation. Globalisation as a phenomenon has been discussed by many writers -some supporting it while others pointing to its weaknesses. Jagdish Bhagwati has defended globalisation as a liberating force for national economies stuck in rigid governmental controls. He has primarily focused on economic globalisation. The issues related to liberalisation, privatisation have been discussed at length. However, the issues related to cultural globalisation and consequent linguistic and cultural hegemonies have received the attention of academia and policy-makers quite late. Off late this issue has been discussed from various standpoints. One area of concern is whether the English language is the principal tool of cultural globalisation and whether it is being used to promote a new form of imperialism. Robert Phillipson[22] has discussed at length how English language has become the tool of cultural globalisation. He explains the ideology and economics behind the expansion of the English language. He argues that there is a well designed project to establish English as the world Language and how it threatens the future of other languages in the world. Looking at the way in which English is promoted all over the world including in India, one tends to agree with his observations. However, it can also be argued that this kind of generalisation perpetuates the myth of English as a killer language which is far from reality.

One of the major concerns of contemporary times has been the use of information and communication technology for the spread of a language. It is followed by the debates on localisation as the tool of empowerment of languages. Whether production of software technologies in a particular language leads to hegemonising of that language and disempowerment of others has been discussed by many. This is a welcome sign in the sense that language issues have enmeshed with technology and therefore it is difficult to study them in isolation.

Various nations have established agencies for the development of their languages. This along with the fear of endangerment of a language seems to be the common trend across the globe.

1.2 Hypothesis and Research Questions

The above survey of relevant literature poses a few question which pertain to this research:

- What is the relationship between language as a marker of identity and the politics that uses language as an instrument?
- What are the various ways of mobilisation to foster linguistic identities?
- What role does the state play in promotion of a language in various domains of social life?
- What is the impact of globalisation on identities in general and linguistic identities in particular?
- What are the possible ways in which linguistic identities will be restructured by globalisation and consequent Information and Communication Technology revolution?

The present research aims at answering these and some other questions in the context of Maharashtra. While it is necessary to understand the global scenario as far as identity construction and identity politics is concerned, one has to be careful about the specific language scenario. It is in this context that the present study aims at

Studying the impact of;

(i) The formation of Maharashtra State and;

(ii) Political parties engaged in mobilisation on the basis of Marathi language;

(iii) Civil society organisations working for the promotion of Marathi in various domains on the status of Marathi language, its development and use at various levels;

(iv) The forces of globalisation on political parties, civil society organisations and the state in the setting of linguistic agenda post-globalisation.

Through this research, I intend to address the following issues:

1. Politics of Marathi linguistic identity has been an instrument of achieving political ends; and does *not necessarily* result in the protection, upliftment, development, and wider use of Marathi language.
2. With the onslaught of globalisation, nativistic mobilisation based on the idea of the Other may not work as a mobilisational strategy.
3. Issues of language planning, shift and survival are integral to a contemporary and pro-active agenda of identity politics based on language.
4. An entire project, involving concerted efforts at the level of the government and complemented by similar private efforts is needed to prevent the declining use of Marathi language and promote its further development.
5. This would require redesigning of the Marathi ideology in a manner that it takes cognisance of the contemporary internal and external challenges.

1.3 Methodology

I intend to carry out the research by analysing the Samyukta Maharashtra Movement, Shivsena, Maharashtra Navnirman Sena and contemporary civil society movements focused on language issues. While doing this I draw upon the existing published material on these movements. However, much needs to be written to have a comprehensive understanding of these movements. I have made an attempt to fill up the gap by interviewing some of the stakeholders and interpreting material not used by researchers so far. I also intend to gather opinions of various stakeholders of language politics like leaders of political parties in Maharashtra, leaders of civil society organisations working for Marathi, office bearers of literary organisations, non-resident Maharashtrians or Maharashtrians staying in other parts of the country, members of the media, Marathi and non-Marathi youth, members of the academia. Through the answers to these questionnaires, I will be able to get a feedback about the nature of politics of Marathi that is desirable and viable in the days to come.

It is through answers to these questions that this thesis will evolve. Unfortunately, major research on linguistic politics looks at events in binaries. It is therefore necessary to break the mould and have a fresh look at the events, issues and ideas surrounding language politics in Maharashtra. Let us now try and understand the key concepts and the framework for analysis.

Notes and References

1. There is plethora of writing on the various dimensions of language politics in India. E.g. in his Politics of India after independence, Paul Brass has analysed the linguistic dimension of politics. Similarly, in their review of post independence politics, Bipin Chandra and others have dealt with language politics in India. However, there are not many books that exclusively deal with language politics in India. The most recent being, Language and Politics in India edited by Asha Sarangi. (Can't make out where it fits).
2. Pendse, Lalji, *Maharashtrache Mahamanthan*, 2nd edition, (Mumbai, Lokwangmay Griha, May 2010).
3. Phadke, Dr Y.D, *Politics and language*: (Mumbai Himalaya Publishing House).
4. Dr Phadke consciously wrote the books in Marathi. He believed that a researcher has the responsibility to produce knowledge in his own language. It is noteworthy that after writing his thesis on Samyukta Maharashtra Movement in English, Dr Phadke had proved his credentials as a researcher in the discipline of political science. He wrote extensively in Marathi with the belief that dissemination of knowledge in Marathi would lead to inspiring the masses to think, thus evolving a more broad based discourse on language politics in Marathi. The author strongly believes that although writing in English is necessary for engaging with those researchers who are not well versed in Marathi, the researcher has a primary responsibility to produce knowledge in his or her language. Besides empowering the language, this also restrains the hegemony of the English language by providing a level playing field to other competing languages.
5. Katzenstein, Mary Fainsod, *Ethnicity and Equality: The Shiv Sena Party and Preferential Policies in Bombay* (Cornell University Press, 1979).

6. The demand of Shivsena was to limit the definition of Marathi to those who are born in Maharashtra and whose mother tongue is Marathi. There was an uproar in the parliament over this demand and it was perceived to be exclusionist. Therefore, the Shivsena demand was diluted and the 15 years residence clause was introduced. Recently, Maharashtra Navnirman Sena raised the demand of preferential treatment to Maharashtrians especially in the context of migrant population of North India. This has been an ongoing debate across India.
7. Gupta, Dipankar, *Nativism in a metropolis: Shivsena in Bombay*, (Mumbai, Manohar, 1982).
8. By this time a major document on the movement 'Maharashtrache Mahamanthan' a diary of the movement written by Lalji Pendse had already been published. It documented the various concerns of the leaders of the Samyukta Maharashtra Movement, one of which was employment. A section of the leadership had realised that if the issue of employment to Maharashtrians is not taken seriously, it would jeopardise the movement. Unfortunately, due to infightings within the Samiti, this issue was sidelined. After the dissolution of the Samiti, there was no political agency that could be looked up to with hope. It is in this vacuum that Shivsena gained prominence in such a short period. Ironically, the above mentioned pioneering books do not pay adequate attention to the resources on the movement available in Marathi. That is a major weakness in the sense that one does not get an insight into the functioning of the Marathi mind.
9. Basu, Amruta and Kohli Atul (Ed.), *Community Conflicts and the State in India* – (OUP, 1998).
10. Purandare, Vaibhav, *The Sena Story* –(Mumbai Business Publications Inc, 1999).
11. Akolkar, Prakash, *Jai Maharashtra, Ha Shivsena Navacha Itihas ahe* (Mumbai, Prabhat Prakashan, 1998).
12. Vora, Rajendra and Palshikar Suhas, *Maharashtratil Sattantar* (Granthali, Mumbai 1996).
13. Dr Palshikar, Suhas (Ed.) *Maharashtratil Sattasangharsha'* (Samakalin Prakashan, Pune, 2007).
14. Hansen, Thomas Blom – *Urban violence in India: Identity politics, Mumbai and the postcolonial city*, (Permanent black, 2001).
15. Joshi, Manohar, *Shivsena – Kaal, Aaj, Udya - History of Shivsena from 1966*, (Mumbai, Prabodhan Prakashan 2008).
16. Joshi, Manohar, *Shivsenechi Nirmiti, Waadh, Swarup, Yashapayash ani Bhartiya Rajkarnatil Shivseneche Bhavitavya Yacha Vishleshanatmak Abhyas (Analytical study of the emergence, growth, nature, success and failure and future in national politics of Shivsena)* (University of Mumbai, Rajiv Gandhi centre for contemporary studies, 2009).

17. Gupta, Jyotirindra Das, *Language Conflict and National Development: Group Politics and National language policy in India.* (University of California Press, 1970).
18. King, Robert D, *Nehru and the Language Politics of India* (OUP, 1997).
19. Chandra, Bipin et. al. (ed.), *India after independence 1947-2000* (2000, Penguin books).
20. Rahman, Tariq, *Language and politics in Pakistan*: (Orient Longman 2007).
21. Ghosh, Partha S., *Ethnicity versus Nationalism – The Devolution discourse in Sri Lanka*, (Sage 2003).
22. Phillipson, Robert, *Linguistic Imperialism,* 1992 & *Linguistic imperialism continued* (Orient Black Swan, 2009).

Chapter 2

Framework for Analysis

This chapter attempts to understand the constitutional provisions about language and their impact on language policies and politics in India. It also makes a brief review of the idea of globalisation and its relationship with politics of linguistic and cultural identity. The chapter begins with constitutional provisions about language and will then narrate the efforts of the union government to promote Hindi as the official language of the Union.

2.1 Constitution and the Considerations of Language

The Constitution of India reflected the aspirations of the people who fought for the independence of the country. Even during the freedom struggle, people belonging to various linguistic communities were demanding reorganisation of the country on linguistic basis. (This is discussed in detail in the chapter on Samyukta Maharashtra Movement)Although the process of linguistic reorganisation of states continued till the early 1970s, the reorganisation of states and formation of smaller states continues even today. The constituent assembly did deliberate the issue of language. Granville Austin has said that the issue of official language of the union was one of the highly debated issues during the constituent assembly deliberations. The Constitution of India mentions Hindi as the official language of the Union and English as the associate official language. Nowhere in the Constitution do we see the word 'National Language'. One thing is clear that our constitution makers have desisted from using the provocative word 'National Language' and instead settling for the tactful euphemism 'official language.'[1] The Eighth Schedule of the Indian Constitution includes 22 languages.[2]

The constituent assembly debated for six weeks the choice for national and/or official language[s] in India. There were controversies about link language, official language and the choice and retention of the national language. The formula providing for Hindi in the Devnagri script to be an official language of the Indian Union along with the continuation of the English language for a period of 15 years from the commencement of the constitution was a result of intense debate.[3]

Official Language Act of 1963 stipulated that English would remain alongside Hindi as an official language of the Union. The Official Language Amendment Act of 1967 guaranteed that English would continue as associate official language indefinitely with the provision that, the state governments, if they so desire have the power to use Hindi in place of English as an official and link language.[4]

Although a section of Hindi supporters believed that Hindi should be the National language and should, soon replace English from its place of prominence, This claim was seldom accepted by supporters of other languages especially those from the southern states. These people argued that all other regional languages should have the status of national language as much as and equal to Hindi. The supporters of English on the contrary argued that English should continue as the de facto national language for a much longer period and should be replaced gradually and with caution.

2.2 Constitutional Provisions

Formation of States

Official website of the Government of India gives details of the provisions about creation of the states and use of languages.

Article 2 of the Constitution of India states that the Parliament may by law admit into the Union, or establish, new States on such terms and conditions as it thinks fit.[5]

Article 3 states that Parliament may by law—

(a) Form a new State by separation of territory from any State or by uniting two or more States or parts of States or by uniting any territory to a part of any State;

(b) Increase the area of any State;

(c) Diminish the area of any State;

(d) Alter the boundaries of any State;

(e) Alter the name of any State.[6]

These provisions form the basis of linguistic reorganisation of states; as well as the creation of new states.

Linguistic Rights of the people

Part III of the Constitution that includes fundamental rights discusses language and cultural rights of people. Article 29[7] of the Indian Constitution is about protection of interests of minorities. It says that any section of the citizens residing in the territory of India /any part thereof, having a distinct language; script or culture of its own shall have the right to conserve the same. However, these rights are not restricted only to the section on fundamental rights which would be clear from the provision mentioned below.

Article 350(a) is about Facilities for instruction in mother-tongue at primary stage. It states that, It shall be the endeavour of every State and of every local authority within the State to provide adequate facilities for instruction in the mother-tongue at the primary stage of education to children belonging to linguistic minority groups; and the President may issue such directions to any State as he considers necessary or proper for securing the provision of such facilities it provides for facilities of instruction through the mother-tongue at the primary stage of education.[8] If Articles 29 and 350A are read together, *the focus of the constitution makers on education in mother tongue becomes clear.*[9]

Language of the Parliament and State Legislatures

Article 120 deals with the Language to be used in the Parliament. Its clause 1 states that, business in Parliament shall be transacted in Hindi or in English. However, the presiding officer of the house may permit any member who cannot adequately express oneself in Hindi or in English, to address the house in his/her mother tongue. However, clause (2) of Article 120 expects that the use of English would automatically cease fifteen years after the commencement of the Constitution of India. Article 210 deals with the language to be used in the state legislature. It provides for the business in the legislature of a state to be transacted in the official language/s of the state or in Hindi or in English. It further states that the presiding officer of the house may permit any member who cannot adequately express oneself in any of the languages aforesaid, to address the house in his/her mother tongue.[10]

Thus, under Article 210, all states have the right to decide their own official language and conduct the business of their respective legislatures in that language. After linguistic reorganisation, states have adopted one or more official language. Some states have also been using English as the official language.

Official language of the Union

Under Article 343(1) Hindi in Devnagari script has been adopted as the official language of the Union. 343 (2) provides for continued use of English for upto 15 years after the commencement of the Constitution. 343 (3) empowers the Parliament to make law providing for the use of the English language for such purposes as may be specified in the law. Article 344 deals with a Commission and Committee of Parliament on official language.[11]

Regional Languages

Article 345 deals with the Official language/s of a State. It states that subject to the provisions of Articles 346 and 347, the legislature of a State may by law adopt any one or more of the languages in use in the State or Hindi as the Language or Languages to be used for all or any of the official purposes of that State: Provided that, until the Legislature of the State otherwise provides by law, the English language shall continue to be used for those official purposes within the State.

Article 346 provides for Hindi and English to be the languages for Communication between one State and another or between a State and the Union. Article 347 deals with the Special provision relating to language spoken by a section of the population of a State. It states that on a demand being made in that behalf the President may, if he is satisfied that a substantial proportion of the population of a State desire the use of any language spoken by them to be recognised by that state, direct that such language shall also be officially recognised throughout that State or any part thereof for such purpose as he may specify.

Language of the Supreme Court, High Courts etc.

Article 348 provides for English as the official language of the Supreme Court and High Courts. Article 348(2) empowers the Governor with the prior consent of the President to authorise the use of Hindi language, or any other used for any official purposes of the state in proceedings in the High Court having its principal seat in that State:[12] This clause however does not apply to any judgment, decree or order passed or made by such High Court.

Special directives related to language

Article 350 deals with Language to be used in representations for redressal of grievances. It states that every person shall be entitled to submit a representation for the redressal of any grievance to any officer or authority of the Union or a State in any of the languages used in the Union or in the State, as the case may be.

Article 350B provides for a special officer for linguistic minorities. It is the duty of the Special Officer to investigate all matters relating to the safeguards provided for linguistic minorities under this Constitution and report to the President which shall to be laid before each House of Parliament and sent to the Government of the States concerned. Although report of the Special Officer for linguistic minorities is tabled before the Parliament every year, it is observed that hardly any action is taken on these reports.[13]

Article 351 is a Directive for development of the Hindi language. The purpose is to ensure that India has a link language, even if there is no consensus on the national language. It may be noted that Mahatma Gandhi had criticised the dominance of English and the consequent marginalisation of Indian languages. He criticised our educated elites for ignoring their own languages. He also resented the fact that Indian elites made their best contributions in English language.[14] If Gandhi had more influence, the Constitution would have had more proactive provisions regarding the development of Indian languages in the Indian Constitution.

Linguistic communities especially from the South India were worried about the dominance of Hindi. To counter the uncompromising approach of the Hindi supporters they supported the continuation of English as the associate official language of the Union of India. In 1965, when the constitutional deadline of 15 years was over, the Government of India planned to replace English with Hindi. There was such an outrage in Northern as well as southern states that the Government had to withdraw the proposal and Continue Hindi as the official language of the Union and English as the associate official language of the union.[15] Since then no effort has been made by the Union Government to replace English. The focus has been to enhance the scope of usage of Hindi through various institutional mechanisms.

2.3 The Official Languages Act and Consequent Policies

The Official Languages Act was passed in 1963.[16] This was followed by the Official Languages (Use for Official Purposes of the Union) Rules; 1976.These rules are applicable to the entire country except the State of Tamil Nadu.

The Department of official language

The Department of official language was established within the Ministry of Home Affairs of the Union Government in June 1975. It looks after the promotion of Hindi. Its aim is to ensure compliance of the constitutional and legal provisions regarding official language and to promote the use of Hindi for the official purposes of the Union.[17]

A careful review of the functions of the Department of language reveals that the Central Government has seriously taken upon itself the task of promotion of Hindi language. The creation of Central Secretariat Official Language Service is a major step whereby a dedicated cadre is created for the promotion of a language. However, the existence of a Central Translation Bureau gives credence to the assumption that laws of the parliament are made in English first and then translated into Hindi. This violates the sanctity of the official language.[18] A good step in the promotion of Hindi is the establishment of Salahkar Samitis or advisory committees in different ministries or departments. One cannot be sure about the utility of these committees.[19]

The establishment of regional implementation mechanism and Parliamentary Committee for inspecting and recommending the use of official language are an important feature of the department. It is not clear however whether members from the non-Hindi region get adequate representation. It would be worthwhile knowing the mandate of the committee and the frequency of its reports.[20] The implementation of these reports may not be done sincerely as it appears from a range of grievances by the Hindi supporters. However, the high profile nature of this committee in itself may be a catalyst in the promotion of Hindi language.[21] A significant but generally ignored provision is that of prior approval of the President for authorising the limited use of a language, other than English, in the proceedings in the High Court of a State. This is included in Article 348(2) of the Constitution. The provision is significant in the sense that it gives a space to regional languages to enter the domain of judiciary. Although the constitution makers were in favour of continuation of English as the language of higher judiciary, they did understand the changed context of a democratic multilingual polity where the demand for enhanced use of regional languages was bound to be raised. Especially after the linguistic reorganisation of states, regional languages got a boost and the above mentioned provision was put to use in many states beginning from the states of North India. Hindi has been declared as the authorised language of High Courts in states of Uttar Pradesh, Bihar, Madhya Pradesh, and Rajasthan. Taking a cue the states of Tamil Nadu and West Bengal (now Pashchimbanga) have passed a resolution in their respective Assemblies to make Tamil and Bengali the authorised languages of their respective high courts and awaiting the Centre's consent.[22]

Despite an elaborate mechanism for the enhancement of the use of Hindi in various domains, Hindi has not become the lingua franca of India. It has been challenged by the increasing importance of English and the growing assertion of various linguistic communities in the projection of their languages.

The review of Constitutional Provisions on language as presented above sets the tone for understanding the complexities of the politics of language and the issues related to language planning. While these issues are constantly shaped by the political process in India, another important factor that has been shaping language issues for the last two decades is globalisation. It is dealt with in the next section.

2.4 Globalisation

Globalisation is variously defined in the literature on international relations and political science. Anthony Giddens describes it as the intensification of worldwide social relations which link distant localities in such a way that local happenings are shaped by events occurring many miles away and vice versa.[23] Gilpin says that globalisation is the integration of the world economy.[24] Scholte says that globalisation means deterritorialisation or the growth of supranational relations between people.[25] It has also been described as time space compression. Thus, Globalisation refers to fundamental changes in the spatial and temporal contours of social existence, according to which the significance of space or territory undergoes shifts in the face of a no less dramatic acceleration in the temporal structure of crucial forms of human activity. One of the key impacts of globalisation is that global events can — via telecommunication, digital computers, audiovisual media, rocketry and the like — occur almost simultaneously anywhere and everywhere in the world. Thus, the growth of Information and Communication Technology has contributed to the death of distance and geography.

Globalisation is linked to the growth of social interconnectedness across existing geographical and political boundaries. It should be conceived as a relatively long-term process. In fact globalisation has been considered as a constitutive feature of the modern world, and modern history includes many examples of globalisation. From the time since the world is interdependent and interconnected, we can witness a semblance of globalisation. Anthony McGrew[26] says that globalisation is a process characterised by:

1. A stretching of economic, social and political activities across political frontiers.
2. The intensification or the growing magnitude of interconnectedness in almost every sphere of social existence.
3. The accelerating process of global interactions and processes.
4. Growing extensity, intensity and velocity of global interactions associated with a deepening enmeshment of the local in global.

There are various patterns of contemporary globalisation.[27] They are:

- Economic-patterns of worldwide trade, finance and production are creating global markets and a global capitalist economy.
- Military- global arms trade, the proliferation of weapons of mass destruction, growth of transnational terrorism is an integral part of this process.
- Legal- The expansion of transnational and international law and the creation of new world legal institutions like International Criminal Court.
- Ecological-shared environmental problems from global warming to extension of species and creation of regimes of global environmental governance.
- Cultural-Global diffusion of popular culture leading to a complex mix of homogenisation and increased heterogeneity. Simultaneous reassertion of nationalism, ethnicity and difference.
- Social-Shifting patterns of migration.

For our present study the idea of cultural globalisation is of utmost importance. Cultural globalisation refers to the transmission of ideas, meanings and values across national borders. This process is marked by the spread of commodities and ideologies, which become standardised around the world. Mass consumption serves as a facilitator between different people and cultures around the globe as a result of the exponential growth of the human population. Through technological advancement, culture has been moving beyond borders and boundaries, transforming through locations the shared meanings of culture. The process of sharing the ideas and values of one culture to another ultimately leads to interconnectedness between various populations from diverse cultures. It is this aspect of globalisation that is more relevant to this research. However, it is not possible to look at any aspect of globalisation in isolation. Therefore, the discussion of the impact of cultural globalisation will invariably take into account other facets of globalisation.

While discussing the impact of cultural globalisation, the role and promotion of English can hardly be overstated. The Handbook of Language and Globalisation[28] gives details about the impact of globalisation and why it is necessary to maintain linguistic and cultural diversity through language planning. Tove Skutnabb-Kangas and Robert Phillipson[29] have analysed the endangerment of languages and possible ways to protect Linguistic Human rights. They argue that a number of languages in the world are on the verge of being extinct. They term this linguicide. The growing influence of English as *lingua academia, lingua bellica, lingua culturalis, and lingua economica are signs of* its hegemony and an expression in linguistic Neo-imperialism. They suggest that English is far increasing in its scope because of its increasing assertion through formal education. Deemphasising mother tongue education has contributed majorly to this. Tariq Rahman says that the Pakistani state supports English as the sole medium of higher education on Pakistan's elite. That English as the sole medium of higher education has alienated the elites from the masses.[30]

For the preservation of Hindi, the constitution makers have made elaborate but not really adequate arrangements. However, there are very few provisions for the promotion of the official language of a state. I intend to discuss the reasons of this in the proposed thesis. Terralingua is a movement that focuses on biocultural diversity through its projects and collaborations. Its website says, "People who lose their linguistic and cultural identity may lose an essential element in a social process that commonly teaches respect for nature and the understanding of the natural environment and its processes. Forcing this cultural and linguistic conversion....not only violates their human rights but also undermines the health of the world's ecosystems.[31] Cultural diversity is closely linked to biodiversity. Humanity's collective knowledge of biodiversity and its use and management rests in cultural diversity; conversely conserving biodiversity often helps strengthen cultural integrity and values.

Thus, preservation of languages and developing institutional mechanisms for the same becomes necessary.

2.5 Constitution, Globalisation and Marathi Language

It will be argued in this thesis that the Indian Constitution guarantees the status of minority languages. However, it does not have explicit provisions for the protection of majority languages that have become official languages of various linguistic states after the creation of linguistic states. The reason may be that the Congress leadership involved in the making of the Constitution had not visualised that the demands for creation of linguistic states would be so widespread and mass based across India. Elaborate mechanisms of language planning may not guarantee the development of a language, yet it would create conducive atmosphere for the various stakeholders in language development to proactively engage with the issue. This however does not negate the need for language planning for the language of the majority and the official language of a state. As far as Maharashtra is concerned, the creation of the state of Maharashtra led to expectations for an improved status for Marathi language. Demand for this led to government initiatives for language planning. A perceived gap between expectations and efforts led to political mobilisations voicing spontaneous anger of the Marathi-speaking people and civil society movements focusing on micro issues of language. Despite this, many problems pertaining to Marathi language and culture remain unresolved.

Marathi has faced internal as well as external challenges. Internally, various dialects of Marathi are struggling for coexistence and accommodation. The discourse on standard and non-standard versions of Marathi language has virtually split the Maharashtrian community along class and caste and sub-regional lines. Although linguistic reorganisation of states created more or less homogeneous states, the political economy of development had different manifestations in different regions within a state. Even in Maharashtra, regional imbalance is a reality. A section of the political leadership from backward areas like Vidarbha is demanding for separate statehood, although the demand does not have mass support.[32] There are demands for creation of smaller states as a tool for overall development of backward regions. Thus, the very idea of one language, one state is under scrutiny. However, even if there would be more states of people speaking the same language are created (in case of this thesis, Marathi); the problems of language would continue to exist. There are demands from various quarters about appointing a second states reorganisation commission.[33] Under these circumstances, the very idea of identity based politics on language may undergo fundamental changes. How these changes will affect Maharashtra's language policy and politics is discussed in later chapters. External challenge is that of migration. Huge influx of migrants to big cities has unsettled the demographic balance. It has created a fear in the minds of the locals that they would be outnumbered and their economic opportunities usurped by outsiders.

Bernard Spolsky[34] says that language policy cannot be studied in isolation because it affects many variables and is in turn affected by many other factors. In countries where problems of poverty, malnutrition, unemployment, gender discrimination exist, usage or non-usage of a language may appear to be a rather non-significant version for some. As far as our discussion on Maharashtra and Marathi is concerned, care has been taken to relate issues of language policy and politics to issues of empowerment of people. This is an attempt to broaden the scope of identity politics based on language so that it becomes proactive and comprehensive.

Before, venturing into this let us try and understand the genesis of language politics in Maharashtra through the Samyukta Maharashtra Movement that led to the creation of the state.

Notes and References

1. Quoted in Sarangee, Asha: *Language and politics in India*, (OUP, New Delhi, 2009, p. 43).
2. Official Website of the Ministry of Law, Government of India.

   http://lawmin.nic.in/olwing/coi/coi-english/Const.Pockper cent202Pg. Rom8Fsss(36).pdf.

These languages are Assamese, Bengali, Bodo, Dogri, Gujarati, Hindi, Kannada, Kashmiri, Konkani, Maithili, Malayalam, Manipuri, Marathi, Nepali, Oriya, Punjabi, Sanskrit, Santhali, Sindhi, Tamil, Telugu, and Urdu.

3. Austin, Granville, *Working a democratic constitution: The Indian experience;* (OUP, Fifth impression, 2001, chapter 6, footnote 33, p.154).
4. http://www.languageinindia.com/april2002/officiallanguagesact.html
5. The full and updated text of the Constitution of India can be found at http://lawmin.nic.in/olwing/coi/coi-english/Const.Pockper cent202Pg.Rom8Fsss(4).pdf
6. *Ibid.*
7. http://indiacode.nic.in/coiweb/welcome.html
8. http://lawmin.nic.in/olwing/coi/coi-english/Const.Pockper cent202Pg.Rom8Fsss(23).pdf
9. Looking at the situation when the Constitution was drafted, it is very obvious that the constitution makers were concerned about the protection of linguistic minorities. After the creation of more or less homogeneous linguistic states, the problem of linguistic minorities has been taken care of in many states. What the constitution makers could not have visualised was that majority languages would also face challenges of survival due to gross negligence on the part of political elites.
10. http://lawmin.nic.in/olwing/coi/coi-english/Const.Pockper cent202Pg.Rom8Fsss(9).pdf
11. It states that such Commission would be constituted by the President after five years and within fifteen years of the commencement of the constitution. It would look into the ways of progressively increasing the use of Hindi and restricting the use of English. Under clauses (4) & (5) a parliamentary committee would be constituted to examine the recommendations of the commission mentioned above.
12. It is through this provision that many states have declared their official languages as the authorised languages of their respective High Courts.
13. A pertinent example closer to Marathi and Maharashtra is about the problems of Marathi speaking people of the disputed border areas of Belgaon, Khanapur etc. Despite regular complaints about the imposition of Kannada, no action has been taken against the Government of Karnataka.
14. Dharmadhikari (Ed), *Gandhi Vichardarshan,* Vol.1, Maharashtra Gandhi Smarak Nidhi Prakashan 3rd Edition, May 1995, pp.130-132.
15. Austin Granville, *Working a democratic constitution: The Indian experience;* OUP, Fifth Impression, 2001.
16. The Official Languages Act, 1963 (As Amended, 1967) (Act No. 19 of 1963). The text can be accessed at the website of the Ministry of Social Justice and Empowerment http://socialjustice.nic.in/olact1963.php

17. As per the Government of India (Allocation of Business) Rules, 1961, this Department has been entrusted with the following items of work: - The details are available on this link. http://rajbhasha.nic.in/
18. This is not an isolated phenomenon. It happens in various states as well Eg. In Maharashtra bills are prepared in English and then translated in Marathi by the Directorate of Language. The translated version is then presented to the legislature as the original one. This is despite unambiguous provisions in the official languages act of 1965 about the language of the legislature. There is tacit consensus among the legislators from different political parties or so it appears. Throughout last three decades they have maintained studied silence on this issue.
19. In an era of coalition politics where the major partner of the coalition needs smaller political parties for survival, language concerns of regional political parties have to be taken into account. Under these circumstances, one can safely argue that such committees may be toothless bodies repeating the rituals year after year.
20. The details about the Committee's mandate and its reports can be found at http://rajbhashasamiti.gov.in/abouteng.htm
21. Whether states can replicate this model and constitute a committee of legislators for the promotion of the official language of the state needs to be probed further.
22. It may be noted that in the same period, the Government of Maharashtra despite demands from language activists did not take any action on the issue. The issue has been amply discussed in judicial conferences across the state. Neither the High Court, nor the State Government seems to be in a hurry on this pressing issue.
23. Giddens, Anthony, *The Consequences of Modernity*. (Cambridge: Polity, 1990).
24. Gilpin, Robert, *Global Political Economy: Understanding the International Economic Order* (Princeton University Press, 2001).
25. Scholte, Jan Aart, *Globalisation: A Critical Introduction* (London: Macmillan 2000).
26. McGrew, Anthony, *Globalisation and Global politics in Baylis John, Smith Steve-The Globalisation of World Politics,* OUP, 2005, pp. 19-40.
27. *Ibid.*
28. Coupland Nikolas, *The Handbook of Language and globalisation* (Wiley-Blackwell, 2010)
29. Tove Skutnabb-Kangas and Phillipson Robert, *The Global politics of Language: Markets, Maintenance, Marginalisation or Murder?* in Coupland Nikolas- *The Handbook of Language and globalisation*-Wiley-Blackwell, 2010, pp.77-100.

30. Full article of Tariq Rahman titled 'Role of English in Pakistan' can be accessed at http://www.tariqrahman.net/language/Roleper cent20ofper cent20Englishper cent20inper cent20Pakistan.htm

    I argue that the problem with India is more or less the same. Using English as the sole language of higher education has led to deprioritisation of Indian languages as far as their economic merit is concerned. Generally the elites educated in a foreign language are not very sensitive to the development of their mother tongues because they don't see any merit in the education of these languages. Political elites have to speak about language issues at least notionally because it is an emotive issue and identity marker that can help in en masse voting. Therefore they do take up issues based on language for political reasons. However, in case of many of them their mother tongues or official languages of their respective states. Looking at the penetration of dynastical politics in India, we see huge influx of family members across political parties. The new generation of entrants with few exceptions is trained in English medium from the primary level. It has altered their sensitivities to such an extent that they have become facilitators and spokespersons of education in English language. Post globalisation education has been commoditised and education through English medium schools has become a booming business. One can safely conclude that the generations of Indian political elites did not do much for their languages because they failed to understand the linkage between language, culture and empowering of a linguistic community through language planning. The new entrants are in a different ideological mode altogether where preservation of Indian languages through conscious language planning is a distant agenda.
31. http://www.terralingua.org/
32. For a detailed discussion on various issues of the Vidarbha problem, see weekly Saadhana issue of 14.08.2010.
33. Report of a two-day international seminar on 'Re-Envisioning States Reorganisation in India', organised by department of political science, faculty of social sciences, Banaras Hindu University (BHU), Quoted in Times of India, Feb 22, 2012.
34. Spolsky Bernard, *Language Policy :Key issues in sociolinguistics,* (Cambridge University Press, 2004).

Chapter 3

Samyukta Maharashtra Movement

The movement for the creation of Unified or Samyukta Maharashtra is a major event not only in the history of Maharashtra, but also in the post-independent history of India. As a movement it drew attention of people across the country. It attracted extreme reactions from different political quarters. The protracted struggle was a manifestation of various socio economic and politico-cultural forces shaped over a period of time. There are a few key themes of the movement. They are:

- Arousal of Marathi consciousness for the creation of a linguistically and culturally homogeneous state of Marathi speaking people. In the process various Marathi speaking regions had to arrive at a consensus about the arrangement of sharing of power after the creation of the state.
- Influence of the largely non-Marathi trader/ capitalists in Bombay on the issue of the status of Bombay City. The Congress high command under the influence of the Bombay capitalists on the issue of inclusion of the city of Bombay in Maharashtra
- Subsequent formation of a coalition of Non-Congress parties to force the Parliament change its decision on the issue of bilingual Bombay state. Congress had thumping majority in the Parliament. Members of the Coalition recognised Samyukta Maharashtra Samiti had negligible

Parliamentary presence. Therefore, they had to use politics of agitation to force the Parliament to revert the decision.

3.1 Demand for Linguistic States and Demand for Maharashtra

The British had divided India into administrative provinces to suit their administrative convenience. It depended on the order of conquest/occupation. Even before independence, a number of linguistic communities had demanded for homogenous regions. In his 1909 dispatch, Lord Hardinge had mentioned about the 'Bihar for Biharis' conflict. The Hindi speaking Bihar region was included in the Bengal province. He had warned the British about the need for creation of homogenous regions.[1] In 1906 Benares Congress, Tilak spoke about Swadeshi, National education, Swarajya and Boycott. While elaborating on his ideas he said that education should be given in the mother tongue up to the university level, government business should be conducted in the local language of the people.[2]

In the 1917 special session of the Congress at Calcutta, Pattabhi Sitaramayya demanded the creation of a separate province of Andhra. Most of the Congress leaders including Annie Besant, Madanmohan Malaviya, and Mahatma Gandhi criticised him for this demand. However, Lokmanya Tilak forcefully supported his demand and the Congress constitution was modified to create an Andhra Province. While accepting the presidentship of the All India Home Rule League, Gandhi vouched for the linguistic redistribution of Provinces.[3]

The Montague-Chelmsford reforms of 1919 recommended that administrative regions of British India will need to be redesigned on the basis of language, cultural homogeneity and administrative convenience. It conceded the need to redistribute provinces wherever it was necessary and suggested that it could be attempted through a process of consent.[4] Nehru Commission report of August 1928 advocated the cause of linguistic reorganisation of states. However, the support of the Nehru Committee was not unreserved on linguistic provinces.[5]

In a prayer meeting on 25.01.1948 Gandhi[6] suggested that linguistic states are part of the principles of the Congress. He said, "If regional languages have to be developed at the optimum level, it is imperative that we reorganise provinces on a linguistic basis. The national language of the country can't replace mother tongues of people. It can't become the medium of instruction in the provinces, neither can English...reorganisation of states would contribute to improvisation in Education and commerce."[7] As the Congress had accepted the principle of linguistic organisation, it was only logical that the process should have begun after independence. However, the massacre during partition forced it to change its stand and oppose the demand of linguistic reorganisation of states citing the fear of disintegration of the country. This fear reflected during the debates in the constituent assembly. The supporters of linguistic reorganisation raised this issue during the Constituent Assembly debates, but could not get favourable response from Nehru or Patel. The members of the constituent assembly who supported linguistic reorganisation held a meeting under the chairmanship of Pattabhi Sitaramayya. Bapusaheb Gupte, S K Patil, Keshavrao Jedhe, H V Pataskar, S N Mane were some of the supporters of this conference.[8] On 12th June 1947, a unanimous resolution was passed by these members in which it was suggested that a commission should be appointed for the creation of regions like Andhra Pradesh, Karnataka, Kerala and Maharashtra. On 27th November 1947; Nehru gave a reply to the question on linguistic reorganisation of state in the Constituent Assembly in which he stated that:

1. The decision on linguistic reorganisation of states has to be taken very seriously.
2. Priority should be given to the security and stability of India.
3. It is not possible to restructure provinces on a large scale.
4. A number of boundary commissions will have to be appointed which will be burdensome.

5. The demand for independent Andhra province is valid and such a province can be created with lesser difficulties. However, the final decision about it can be taken only after the country accepts the constitution.
6. There are more difficulties in the creation of Maharashtra and Karnataka. The impact of their separation on the province's economy has to be carefully studied.[9]

3.2 Dar and JVP Commission

Despite Nehru's reluctance, Government of India had to take some steps in the direction of creation of linguistic states. On 17 June 1948, Rajendra Prasad, the President of the Constituent Assembly, set up the Linguistic Provinces Commission (called Dar Commission) to recommend whether the states should be reorganised on linguistic basis or not. The committee included SK Dar (retired Judge of the Allahabad high Court), JN Lal (lawyer) and Panna Lall (retired ICS officer). In its 10 December 1948 report, the Commission recommended that "the formation of provinces on exclusively or even mainly linguistic considerations is not in the larger interests of the Indian nation." It recommended the reorganisation of the provinces of Madras, Bombay and Central provinces and Berar primarily on the basis of geographical contiguity, financial self-sufficiency and ease of administration.[10] While criticising the demand for Unified Maharashtra the report said, 'Maharashtrians are aggressive and feudal in mindset, especially those with the Poona mentality. That's the most dangerous thing among them. Maharashtra has no right over Bombay. It can't be included in one region because it belongs to the entire country.'[11] Dr Y.D. Phadke who has studied the Samyukta Maharashtra Movement has said that irresponsible remarks made by responsible bodies appointed to study the problem of linguistic provinces gave the impression to the Maharashtrians that there was an animus against them.[12] There was outrage in Maharashtra over the decision of the commission and its observations about Maharashtra. The report was rejected by the Congress.

Soon after the report was published, the Congress, at its Jaipur session, set up the "JVP committee" to study the recommendations of the Dar Commission. The committee comprised Jawaharlal Nehru, Vallabhbhai Patel and Congress president Pattabhi Sitaramayya. In its report dated 1 April 1949, the Committee stated that the time was not suitable for formation of new provinces, but also stated "if public sentiment is insistent and overwhelming, we, as democrats, have to submit to it, but subject to certain limitations in regard to the good of India as a whole." The Committee accepted the demand of the Andhra Province excluding the city of Madras. It also hinted at keeping the city of Bombay separate from Maharashtra.[13] Thus, as far as Maharashtra is concerned, the journey towards statehood was marked by difficulties. Let us now see the various issues that had to be sorted out before the creation of Maharashtra and the efforts of the Marathi speaking people in that direction. Let us look at some of these developments.

3.3 Samyukta Maharashtra: Initial Developments

Maharashtra Sahitya Sammelan held in Mumbai on 16th October 1938 passed a resolution that a unilingual region of Maharashtra should be created by incorporating the Varhad region into it. It was also suggested that the Princely state of Hyderabad be dissolved and after its trifurcation the Marathwada region be incorporated in Maharashtra. After the dissolution of the Portuguese power even Goa be incorporated into the state.[14] In 1938, Datto Waman Potdar spoke about the unification of Maharashtra.[15] The 1939 Sahitya Sammelan at Nagar reiterated the demand for Samyukta Maharashtra. The name Samyukta Maharashtra was popularised from this time onwards.[16] Journalists and writers in Maharashtra issued an appeal in November 1939 to establish 'Samyukta Maharashtra Sabha' to pursue the cause of Samyukta Maharashtra on a sustained basis.[17] In May 1941 'Maharashtra Ekikaran Parishad' (Maharashtra Unification conference) was established.[18]

In the early 1950s, Congressmen in Maharashtra were still involved in the movement for the creation of Samyukta Maharashtra.

Prominent among them was Shankarrao Deo who headed the Samyukta Maharashtra Parishad. He was quite confident that a unified Maharashtra will be created in near future. However, his insistence upon including the city of Bombay in the proposed Maharashtra state brought him in conflict with Sardar Patel and Nehru.[19] Congress leaders like Yashwantrao Chavan were of the opinion that Samyukta Maharashtra can be achieved only by persuading Nehru and the Congress High Command because the Congress working committee had instructed Congressmen not to join any agitations for the creation of linguistic states. Participation of the Communists in the struggles for reorganisation of states had made the Congress leadership wary of the intentions behind these agitations. Besides the fear of falling out with Nehru, Congressmen in Maharashtra were afraid of doing anything that would strengthen the Communists.[20] Therefore, with few exceptions the Congress Party in Maharashtra distanced itself from the Samyukta Maharashtra Movement. However, Congressmen in Gujarat did join the Mahagujarat Parishad that fought for the creation of Gujarat. In fact, the leaders of the Samyukta Maharashtra Samiti considered their struggle as complimentary and supported it.[21]

3.4 States Reorganisation Commission's (SRC) Report and its Aftermath

Andhra Pradesh was created after large scale violence that followed the death of Potti Sriramalu (who began a fast unto death for the demand of creation of Andhra Pradesh and died on the 52nd day of his fast). After the creation of Unilingual Andhra Pradesh, demands for the creation of other linguistic states were also put forward. A commission headed by Fazal Ali and consisting of members like Sardar Panikkar and H. N. Kunzru was appointed in 1953 to recommend the redrawing of boundaries on linguistic basis. This commission is also known as States Reorganisation Commission. While deciding about states, the SRC was in favour of bigger states. It opined that smaller states have more non-productive expenses. Bigger states can undertake energy generation and river valley development projects. The commission also opined that the states can't be given right to self determination. If history is given more importance while reorganising states, it would lead to revivalism and parochialism. When the report of the Commission was published in 1955, it rejected the demand of creation of Maharashtra with the inclusion of the city of Bombay. It recommended the creation of bilingual state of Bombay including the Gujarati-speaking areas of Kutch and Saurashtra. Belgaum and the other Marathi speaking regions were included in Karnataka. A separate state of Vidarbha was proposed.[22] The report of the Commission was a disappointment for the people of Maharashtra not only because it rejected the demand for Samyukta Maharashtra, but because it did not apply the same criteria which it applied while creating other linguistic states. There was outrage against the recommendations of the SRC. People came out on the streets in the city of Bombay agitating against the recommendations of the report. It was then that the then Chief Minister Morarji Desai gave orders to fire on the agitating people. Shoot at sight and shoot to kill was the instruction to the police officers.[23] In the indiscriminate firing ordered by Morarji Desai's government, 106 people lost their lives. This was a turning point in the struggle for creation of Maharashtra. Henceforth the Congress in the state as well as the Centre was completely alienated from the movement that was run by the Samyukta Maharashtra Samiti.

3.5 Major Issues in the Creation of Maharashtra

There were many hurdles to the creation of Unified Maharashtra. They are listed below.

- ***The inclusion of the city of Bombay in Maharashtra***

There were multiple opinions about the city. Patel and Gandhi were not in favour of including the city in Maharashtra whereas Nehru wanted it to be a centrally administered territory. Both Patel and Gandhi died before the agitation for Samyukta Maharashtra began. However, when the Marathi-speaking people rejected the recommendations of the SRC, Nehru suggested a plan in which the City of Bombay was to be a Union Territory. This was a step to maintain its cosmopolitan character. The Non-Marathi capitalist class backed by the Bombay Pradesh Congress Committee President S.K. Patil was against the inclusion of the city in Maharashtra.[24] During the visit of the Dar Commission as well as the States Reorganisation Commission, the influential sections like the Indian Merchants' Chambers, Bombay Citizens Committee, some academicians from the University of Bombay submitted memorandums against the inclusion of the city of Bombay in Maharashtra. In his memorandum submitted to Dar Commission,[25] Dr Ambedkar argued for Maharashtra as a linguistic state and why it was necessary to include the city of Bombay in Maharashtra. He said, 'Maharashtra and Bombay are not merely inter-dependent, they are really one and integral. Severance between the two would be fatal to both. The sources of water and electricity for Bombay lie in Maharashtra. The intelligentsia of Maharashtra lives in Bombay. To sever Bombay from Maharashtra would be to make the economic life of Bombay precarious and to dissociate the masses of Maharashtra from its intelligentsia without whose lead the masses of Maharashtra will be nowhere.'

- When the States Reorganisation Commission proposed a bigger bilingual state, in a scathing attack[26] on the proposition Ambedkar said, 'The present State of Bombay is the best illustration of the failure of democracy in a mixed State. I am amazed at the suggestion made by the States Reorganisation Commission that the present Bombay State should be continued as it is to enable us to gain experience of how a mixed State flourishes. With Bombay as a mixed State for the last 20 years, with the intense enmity between the Maharashtrians and Gujaratis, only a thoughtless or an absent-minded person could put forth such a senseless proposal.'
- By this time the Congress leadership in Maharashtra had come to the conclusion that they will have to accept the

bigger bilingual state for all practical reasons. It's only when its functioning became unviable and the Congress suffered heavy losses in the 1957 elections, the Congress High Command had to take note of the mounting dissent of the people. Indira Gandhi as the president of the Congress Party played a key role in convincing Nehru about the need to break up the bilingual state. Nehru ensured that Congress will remain in majority in both the states after bifurcation.[27] When the new state was announced, Nehru wanted to name it as Bombay state. Due to the stiff opposition of the Samyukta Maharashtra Samiti, he had to reluctantly accept the name Maharashtra.[28] Thus, the demand for the inclusion of the city of Bombay was almost central to the movement led by the Samyukta Maharashtra Samiti.

- ***The dissolution of Nizam's Hyderabad state and the inclusion of Marathi-speaking areas of Marathwada in Maharashtra***

In Nizam's Hyderabad, Urdu was declared as the Medium of instruction for school as well as university education. It was the language of state administration and judiciary. The regional languages were actively suppressed. After the police action in Hyderabad in 1948, there was growing demand that the Kannada, Marathi and Telugu speaking regions of the Hyderabad state should be included in the adjoining unilingual states of Karnataka, Maharashtra and Andhra Pradesh respectively.[29] Nehru and Maulana Azad were in favour of retaining the status quo as they considered the Hyderabad state as the stronghold of Islamic culture.[30] A movement under the leadership of Ramanand Tirth worked for the inclusion of Marathwada in Maharashtra. In a session of All India Congress Committee held at Hyderabad, Tirth strongly demanded for trifurcation of the erstwhile Nizam state which Nehru fiercely opposed.[31] Some of the industrialists from Hyderabad and Varhad were pushing the idea of a separate region consisting of some districts of Marathwada and Nagpur region. However, leaders of Marathwada like Uddhavrao Patil relentlessly fought for the creation of unified Maharashtra and the inclusion of Marathwada in it.

- ***Negotiations with the leadership of Vidarbha so that some of them demanding for Separate Mahavidarbha state give up that demand and join Maharashtra***

The region of Vidarbha was part of the erstwhile Central Provinces. The Marathi-speaking region of the central province was separated from the central province on 1st October 1938.[32] Although efforts were on for the creation of Unified Maharashtra, looking at the hurdles in its way on 8th August 1947, leaders of various regions of the Marathi speaking area signed the Akola Pact. One of the hidden clauses of the Akola Pact was that Samyukta Maharashtra Parishad should support the creation of independent Vidarbha in case the demand for the creation of unilingual state of Maharashtra with Mumbai is not accepted or postponed due to political exigencies. The leaders of the Samyukta Maharashtra Movement realised that more comprehensive understanding of power sharing with the Vidarbha leaders was needed if they wanted to achieve unified Maharashtra with Vidarbha. Therefore, on 28th September 1953, Nagpur Pact[33] was signed nullifying the Akola Pact. Salient features of this pact were as follows:

1. For the purpose of development and governance, Mahavidarbha, Marathwada and rest of Maharashtra would be considered as three units.
2. Special attention would be given to Marathwada keeping in mind its backwardness.
3. Nagpur bench of the High Court will work for Mahavidarbha. Proper representation would be given to people from Vidarbha and Marathwada while selecting judges for the High Court.
4. Decentralisation would be the motto of the government. The importance of Nagpur is well recognised and would be continued even after the creation of unified Maharashtra. All the government offices would be shifted to Nagpur for a specific period. At least one session of the state legislature would be held at Nagpur.[34]

The SRC accepted the demand of separate Vidarbha. Due to the opposition of the Marathi-speaking people to the recommendations of the SRC report, the state of Vidarbha could not come into existence. Within Vidarbha, there were Congressmen who supported joining Maharashtra. They included Vasantrao Naik and later on Marotrao Kannamwar. Brijlal Biyani and Bapuji Ane were supporters of separate Vidarbha state. Biyani argued that if there can be three Hindi-speaking states, why can't we have two Marathi-speaking states? He also argued that bigger unilingual states would be a threat to the Union of India.[35] On 21st July 1958, the supporters of separate Vidarbha organised Nag-Vidarbha Parishad in Akola. It was inaugurated by Bapuji Ane. He suggested that Nag-Vidarbha should be created as a separate state as per the recommendation of the state reorganisation commission. Ane and his supporters were apprehensive that Brahmins of Pune will dominate unilingual Maharashtra.[36] But they had not realised that Brahmins had ceased to be a dominant force in the Congress during the 1950s, and were already replaced by Marathas.

- ***Inclusion of Goa in Maharashtra after its liberation***

Goa was under Portuguese control since the 17th century. After the independence of the country from the British, there was growing demand for liberation of Goa. After the police action in Hyderabad, it was expected that Nehru will order similar action in Goa. But On 10th July 1946, Nehru told reporters, "Goa is just like a wart on the face of India. It won't take much time to crush it. Therefore, there is no need of a movement for liberation of Goa."[37] In 1954, Praja Socialist Party Workers from Maharashtra and Gujarat took lead in establishing Goa liberation support committee. Leaders like Senapati Bapat, Nanasaheb Gore participated in the struggle. The Portuguese authorities attacked the peaceful satyagrahees mercilessly. Nehru talked of peace and patience and described Goa as an old tumor.[38] When Maharashtrians started participating in the Goa liberation movement in large numbers Nehru criticised that the agitation is going in the wrong direction. Even before the liberation of Goa, the issue of its inclusion in Maharashtra was widely discussed. Gomantak Marathi Sahitya Sammelan was held first in 1947. It was demanded that Konkani being a dialect of Marathi, Konkani speakers should be identified as Marathi speakers in census, after the linguistic reorganisation of states, and after the liberation of Goa, Goa should be included in Maharashtra.[39]

Goa was not liberated until 1961. Maharashtra had already come into existence in 1960. After the liberation of Goa, opinion poll was held for its merger with Maharashtra. Bhausaheb Bandodkar, the leader of Maharashtravadi Gomantak Party was a strong supporter of Goa's merger in Maharashtra. However, he did not succeed in this venture.[40] One of the reasons for a strong opposition to the merger with Maharashtra was the fear of mine owners in Goa that their business will be affected in a large state like Maharashtra. Another reason was the fear of Goa's dominant Saraswat community that they will be dominated by numerically strong Marathas in unified Maharashtra. But the most important fact seems to be the feeling of perceived injustice to Konkani by the speakers of Marathi.[41]

- ***Inclusion of the border areas of Belgaum, Karwar, Nipani, Khanapur, Bidar, Bhalki, Supa, Halyal in Maharashtra by settling the dispute with the state of Mysore***

The Marathi-speaking areas of Belgaum, Karwar, Nipani, Khanapur, Bidar, Bhalki, Supa, and Halyal were given to the Mysore state by the SRC report. This was in complete violation of the principles accepted by SRC regarding linguistic reorganisation. On 25th June 1956, a zonal council that was appointed to settle the boundary dispute between Maharashtra and Karnataka submitted its memorandum and suggested that Marathi-speaking areas in the Mysore state should be included in Maharashtra. It was also suggested that while deciding the boundary, a village should be considered as a unit besides geographical contiguity and the desire of the people.[42] Member of Parliament from Maharashtra Barrister Nath Pai argued in the parliament that the principles of village as a unit, majority of a linguistic community, geographical contiguity and the desire of people should be followed to resolve the border dispute.[43] However, this was not done. The issue remains unresolved even today. Presently a case in this issue is pending in the Supreme Court.

- ***Including the Dangs district bordering Gujarat in Maharashtra, since Dangi was a dialect of Marathi***

The issue of Dang was a matter of heated debate between the Gujaratis and Maharashtrians. Till 1903, the administration of the Dang region was carried out in Marathi and the government documents were written in the Modi script. Sane Guruji in the 30th April 1949 issue of Sadhana has written on this debate and especially on the linguistic aspect of it. He said that the Warli community from Dang clearly mentions that Gujarat is beyond the Damanganga river and Warlis are not 'Damane' i.e. Gujaratis. Eighty per cent people on the Umbergaon border of Gujarat are Marathi speaking but the moneylenders of the region are Gujaratis. The moneylenders opened schools for their children in the Gujarati medium and then they started claiming that the region is Gujarati. During the meetings in this region Warlis used to lament that the Gujarati moneylenders have taken away all their land, now they are taking away our language as well. Sane Guruji reminded the Gujaratis that the 'Shilalekh (Inscriptions) near the Indragarh fort at Daman is also in Marathi. Gujaratis settled in this region were forced migrants because of the Muslim aggression. Sane Guruji criticised them for taking undue advantage of the gracious behaviour of Maharashtrians.[44] Unfortunately, such emotional appeals did not work in the Dang region. Gujarati medium schools increased in the region. This successful Gujaratisation of Dangs was patronised by the Gujarati speaking ministers of the bilingual Bombay state. During the debate on Dangs, Bhausaheb Hire was actively leading the Marathi speaking community. Maharashtrians were criticised for being linguists and regionalists. While answering to this allegation, Hire wrote in a letter to Mamasaheb Devgirikar,

"We don't feel bad because we are called linguists or regionalists. We are not ashamed of it. Like nationalism, regionalism is bad if it is aggressive. It is good if it is for self defense. We Maharashtrians are asking only for that which belonged to us in the past and which belongs to us even now.[45] Unfortunately, while bifurcating the Bombay state Marathi speaking areas of Dangs were given to Gujarat. It appeared that Yashwantrao Chavan was pressurised by the Congress High Command to take a softer position on Dangs in case the demand for unified Maharashtra with Bombay was accepted. The issue was discussed in a meeting between Raghunathrao Khadilkar, S.M. Joshi, S.A. Dange and Y.B. Chavan.[46] Morarji Desai was against the dissolution of the bigger bilingual state, but had to accept the decision when Chavan, Nehru and G.B. Pant decided in favour of it. Probably, the issue of Dangs was resolved in favour of Gujarat to pacify Morarji Desai.The fact that Morarji Desai had played a major role in Making Chavan the Chief Minister of Bilingual state gives credence to this speculation.

3.6 Samyukta Maharashtra Movement: Success and Failure

After the Samyukta Maharashtra Parishad headed by Shankarrao Deo became defunct, across the political spectrum in Maharashtra need was felt to establish an alternate organisation that will give a platform to the collective resistance of the Marathi speaking people against the recommendations of the SRC. On 6th February 1956, Samyukta Maharashtra Samiti was established in Pune. This was a non-Congress coalition. Eleven parties joined the Coalition. S.M. Joshi of the Praja Socialist Party, S.A. Dange of CPI were the leaders of the movement. Besides them stalwarts like Acharya P.K. Atre, Senapati Bapat, Prabodhankar Thakre, Walchand Kothari, Madhavrao Bagal led the movement. The agenda of the Samiti was to establish unified Maharashtra with the inclusion of the city of Bombay. Samiti forced the state and the central leadership of the Congress to take cognizance of the demand through mass agitations, strikes, Bandhs. The Samiti being a loose coalition of political parties with strong ideological and personal differences, its existence had always been fragile. Although the Samiti got huge success in the 1957 elections riding on the anti-Congress wave, seat sharing among political parties was a tedious task.[47] The success of the Samiti in 1957 was a reflection of people's anger against the Congress for not accepting the genuine demand of unified Maharashtra. By the time people in Maharashtra realised that creation of unified Maharashtra was going to be a reality, the differences within the Samiti had become very visible. Two major issues troubled the Samiti: First, whether to continue the battle for Samyukta Maharashtra relentlessly till the border areas of Belgaon, Karwar etc. are included in Maharashtra and secondly, whether to continue the existence of the Samiti after the creation of Maharashtra. Leaders of the Praja Samajwadi Party like S.M. Joshi and others were arguing that once the task of creating Samyukta Maharashtra is accomplished, the Samiti should cease to exist. Others like Acharya Atre suggested that creation of Maharashtra was just half the work done and the Samiti should continue and evolve as a party so that it emerges as a viable opposition to the Congress.[48] This was an uphill task as it would require political parties with different ideologies to either give up their independent existence or arrive at a Common Minimum Programme (the term frequently used in contemporary coalition politics).When this seemed impossible, Atre used his fiery writings in his famous daily 'Maratha' to criticise individuals and political parties who opposed his suggestion. This further spoiled the atmosphere in the Samiti. Praja Samajwadi Party left the Samiti. Disgruntled Congressmen who had joined the Samiti because of the opposition of Bombay Pradesh Congress Committee Chief S.K. Patil's opposition to the inclusion of the city of Bombay in Maharashtra went back to the Congress. A fragile Samiti was renamed Sampoorna Maharashtra Samiti under the leadership of Dajiba Desai. It was routed in the 1962 elections. Eventually, the differences between Peasants and workers Party and The Communists became so unmanageable that Dajiba Desai had to suspend the work of the Sampoorna Maharashtra Samiti.[49]

Almost five decades after the existence of the Movement, it is appropriate to evaluate its performance.

- **Fragile coalition working under Mass pressure**

Samyukta Maharashtra Samiti was probably the first Non-Congress Coalition in independent India. It had all the elements of a fragile coalition- ideological clashes, personal bickering, pressurising over seat sharing, overzealous and highly independent minded leadership that damaged the organisational apparatus and inability to arrive at a durable consensus on policy issues. The biggest force that kept it together was the desire of the people of Maharashtra to achieve unified Maharashtra with the inclusion of the city of Bombay.

- ***Use of the independent Media***

When the Samyukta Maharashtra Movement under the leadership of the Samiti gathered momentum, it found that except the daily *Navakaal* run by the Khadilkars most of the Marathi and English dailies were against them. The movement needed a newspaper to put forward its view point. Dinu Randive's *Samyukta Maharashtra Patrika* and *Maratha* and *Saanj Maratha* edited by Acharya Atre did this job. In fact, Atre's scathing attack on anyone who opposed the creation of unified Maharashtra not just made it popular, it also kept the momentum of the movement intact. Daily Maratha was started on 15th November 1956 and in 1957 Atre started Saanj Maratha, an eveninger. Maratha was largely funded by the Marathi speaking people who supported the movement. Unfortunately, it did not survive for long after the movement for unified Maharashtra came to an end.

- ***Participation of the cultural representatives of the subaltern class***

Besides newspapers like Maratha, the anger of the Marathi speaking people reflected through the songs and ballads of various folk artists like Shahir Amarshekh, Shahir Annabhau Sathe,

Shahir Gawankar and others. Many of them were members of the Communist party which successfully deployed them for generating mass consciousness on this issue. Through songs like 'Jaaga Maratha Aam, Jamana Badlega' (The common Maratha has awakened and the world will change) common Maharashtrians were mobilised and their confidence was kept intact against all odds. Participation of the cultural elites in a mass movement on this scale has not been seen after the creation of Maharashtra.

- ***Participation of Non Maharashtrians and condemnation of violence***

While the critics of the Samyukta Maharashtra Movement argued that the movement for the creation of Maharashtra represented sectarian interests, the ground reality was different. Even Hindi and Telugu speaking population of the city participated in various phases of the agitation. Non-Marathi leaders like Nausher Bharucha supported the demand for the creation of Maharashtra with Bombay as its capital in the legislature.[50] Even the martyrs in the movement include Non-Maharashtrians. Muslims in Belgaum also petitioned that they want to be a part of Maharashtra. Attempts were made to strain the relationship between Maharashtrians and Gujaratis by spreading rumours about alleged misbehaviour with the Gujarati community. Eventually all these allegations were proved baseless. The Samiti made special efforts to ensure that the movement was not branded as anti-minority.

- ***Role of Congress and Yashwantrao Chavan***

As mentioned earlier, the Congress in Maharashtra with rare exceptions remained away from the movement, although some leaders like Keshavrao Jedhe, Kakasaheb Gadgil sympathised with the movement. S.K. Patil, the leader of the Bombay Pradesh Congress Committee was vehemently against the inclusion of the city of Bombay in Maharashtra. Yashwantrao Chavan worked as the Chief Minister of the bigger bilingual state and made his stand clear that if it comes to choosing between Nehru and Maharashtra, he will choose Nehru. He was heavily criticised by one and all. Govind Talwalkar[51] has provided for a rationale to this controversial statement. He mentions an interview by Chavan to political scientist Jayant Lele in which Chavan said that he had Nehru's leadership and not Nehru as a person in mind. He was sure that Maharashtra with the city of Bombay can be achieved only by remaining in the Congress and through negotiations with the Congress high command. Like Nehru, Chavan was also worried about the growing influence of the Communists in Maharashtra. That hardened his stand against the Samyukta Maharashtra Movement. Even if this is true, it goes without saying that Chavan valued his political position more than the sentiments of the people. He kept on justifying the bigger bilingual state, till the time it became impossible to run the state.

- ***Unfinished agenda***

The Samyukta Maharashtra Movement was a mass agitation that primarily focused on the creation of Maharashtra. Although its leadership proclaimed that they will create socialistic Maharashtra within socialistic India, they could not execute their agenda as the Samiti split and lost political presence. Although the Samiti leadership had talked about the development of Marathi language and culture and employment issues of the Marathi speaking people, they could not evolve a comprehensive agenda for the same. After the creation of Maharashtra, Chavan and Congress dominated the political scene in Maharashtra and Shivsena dominated the space of street politics thus changing the entire discourse of language and culture politics initiated by the Samiti. Had the Samiti sustained as a political force, it is quite possible that the language and culture scene in Maharashtra would have been different.

3.7 Samyukta Maharashtra Movement and the Issue of Marathi Language

The above discussion shows that linguistic reorganisation of states in India was a result of persistent popular demand. It also shows that the creation of the state of Maharashtra was a result of similarly persistent; though much longer struggle by the people. In the context of this thesis, it is important to find out whether and to what extent the Samyukta Maharashtra Movement and its leadership had thought about the status of Marathi language in the new state and the required action for the same. This raises the following questions:

1. What was the understanding of the leadership of the Samyukta Maharashtra Samiti individually and as a coalition as far as the development of Marathi language and culture is concerned?
2. Did it reflect in their programmes or election campaigns?
3. What was the vision of the Samyukta Maharashtra movement as far as the development of the Marathi language and culture after the creation of the state is concerned?
4. What is the legacy of the Samyukta Maharashtra Movement as far as ideas and strategies about the development of Marathi language is concerned?

This section attempts to discuss these issues in details. When the demand for the creation of unilingual states was made, the reason behind it was the unanimous feeling across various linguistic groups that democracy can function better in a unilingual state if the administration of the state would be carried out in the language of the people. This would lead to transparency and better participation of people. It is interesting to note that in the initial phase of the debate over linguistic states, development of regional languages and cultures was not the prime aspect of the agenda.

As far as the demand for Maharashtra was concerned, some of the ideas behind the movement can be found in the conference organised by the Samyukta Maharashtra Samiti on 29th September 1956 in Bombay against the bigger bilingual state.[52] The conference claimed that in the bigger bilingual state the development of the Marathi speaking people suffered and suggested that this development is not possible unless the state becomes unilingual and culturally homogeneous. The conference was a precursor to the elections to be held for the state assembly in 1957. Therefore, the conference advised the Samyukta Maharashtra Samiti to evolve an electoral programme that would chart the economic, social, political and cultural rejuvenation of the Marathi speaking people. The resolution also stated that special efforts should be made for the literary and cultural development of Maharashtra. However, there is no mention of development of Marathi language beyond this. It may be argued that the Samiti did not give much thought to the development of Marathi language and culture during the movement. However, it is understandable because the focus was on the splitting of the bigger bilingual state and forming the unilingual state of Maharashtra with Bombay as its capital. It is also not clear, if the Samyukta Maharashtra Samiti had continued to function after the creation of Maharashtra; it would have evolved its agenda about the development of Marathi language and culture. In reality Samyukta Maharashtra Samiti had begun to split in factions and was eventually routed in the 1962 election. Thus, it could be stated that while the Samyukta Maharashtra Samiti struggled hard for the creation of Samyukta Maharashtra, it was unable to visualise a comprehensive agenda for the development of Marathi language and culture, partly due to its own decline and partly due to its primary focus on the creation of the state.

It does not however mean that the individual leadership of the Samyukta Maharashtra Movement had not given any thought to the issue of the Maharashtrian identity and the development of the Maharashtrian culture. D.K. Bedekar[53] one of the Marxist thinkers said that nationality is regional in nature. Every group of people requires a contiguous and consistent land that they can own. Bedekar in fact elaborated on the ideology behind the creation of Samyukta Maharashtra using the following ideas:

- Marathi speaking region has evolved into a nationality in the course of history on the basis of distinct culture, language and geographical contiguity.

- People in such nationalities can create an accountable and democratic political system on the basis of political independence that they have achieved. This arrangement can be used for their economic and cultural development.
- Thinkers like Chiplunlar, Tilak and Rajwade were aware of the fact that Maharashtra is a nationality and India is a commonwealth of such nationalities. This feeling will evolve with the arousal of national consciousness.
- India of tomorrow will be a federation of independent and autonomous nationalities. All republics within it will be fully autonomous. They will have the freedom to secede if need be.

S.A. Dange the leader of the Communist Party of India (CPI) and one of the prominent leaders of the Samyukta Maharashtra Samiti had discussed the issue at great length. Ashok Chausalkar[54] has discussed Dange's thoughts on this issue in the context of the Samyukta Maharashtra Movement. Being a Communist, Dange was naturally influenced by the ideas of Lenin and Stalin on the issues of nationalism and the role played by language and culture in it. Dange believed in the theory that the Indian federation should be made up of independent and autonomous units. It is on this basis that he supported the demand for Samyukta Maharashtra. Dange believed that there is no contradiction between linguistic nationalism and socialistic culture. He argued that real socialism is not devoid of linguistic identity and culture. He also believed that discrimination and conflicts resulting from capitalistic exploitation and poverty would cease to exist with the end of capitalism. This would contribute to the synergising of linguistic nationalism and socialistic culture. In his speech on Shivaji,[55] Dange elaborated on Shivaji's role in Making Marathi the language of his Swarajya. He says that Shivaji did not waste time by appointing commissions for the use of Marathi. He promptly took the decision. He further added that the contemporary problems of language can also be solved by choosing for the language of the people, because the battle for language is not a technical battle. It is a battle of our collective life.

These thoughts of Dange reflect his deeper understanding of the language and culture question of Maharashtra. It may be said that Dange did not get an opportunity to put his ideas into practice due to marginalisation of the Samyukta Maharashtra Samiti after the creation of Maharashtra.

Other leaders of the movement like S.M. Joshi, Acharya Atre, and Prabodhankar Thakre concentrated their energies on the struggle and did not really discuss the future of Marathi language and culture after the creation of Maharashtra. Lalji Pendse had mentioned about the need to look at the problems of the unemployed Marathi youth, but the issue was not taken very seriously during the movement.[56] This issue was later taken by the Shivsena. Prabodhankar Thakre had written about the huge migration of south Indians in the city of Bombay and consequent injustice to Maharashtrians in his fortnightly magazine 'Prabodhan'[57] in 1922 itself. However, this issue was not raised during the Samyukta Maharashtra movement however. Even this issue was taken by the Shivsena later.

The above discussion would reveal that although the Samyukta Maharashtra Samiti mobilised masses for the creation of Samyukta Maharashtra with Bombay as its capital, it did not spend much of its energies on developing a comprehensive agenda for the development of Marathi language, culture and the empowerment of the Marathi speaking people after the creation of Maharashtra. It is possible to assume that the Samiti considered these as future problems that could be discussed once the creation of the state had been achieved. It is also possible that the general belief was that these problems would be automatically taken care of once the state of Maharashtra is created. Words like language planning, language development were not a part of the political discourse at that time. So it would be anachronistic to expect these things from the Samiti. But it is safe to say that had the Samiti developed a comprehensive agenda on these issues, it would have been a good document to compare with the policies of the later governments. At a later stage it could have also given policy-makers and academicians an opportunity to compare it with the ideology and practice of Shivsena.

Whether, the Samyukta Maharashtra Samiti's leadership could have really done something for the development of Marathi language and culture remains a matter of speculation as the Samiti never ruled the state.

Notes and References

1. Quoted in Pendse Lalji, *Maharashtrache Mahamanthan-* (Lokvangmaygruha Prakashan, Mumbai, 2010, p. 50).
2. Shewalkar, Ram (Ed.), *Lokmanya Tilakanche Nibandh*, (National Book Trust, New Delhi,1996, pp.70-73).
3. Tendulkar, D.G., *Mahatama- Life of Mohandas Karamchand Gandhi* Vol.I, p. 288, Publications Division, New Delhi December 1988. Ironically, in 1949, a high level committee consisting of Jawaharlal Nehru, Vallabh Bhai Patel and Pattabhi Sitaramayya was established to look into the demand for creation of linguistic states. In the report Pattabhi Sitaramayya opposed the creation of Maharashtra as a linguistic state. Sitaramayya said that the demand for Maharashtra was still in its nascent phase. The then Home Minister Govind Vallabh Pant's ancestors originally hailed from Maharashtra. However, while discussing this issue in the parliament, even Pant opposed the creation of Maharashtra.
4. Phadke, Y.D., *Politics and Language*, (Himalaya Publishing House, Bombay, March 1979, p. 3).
5. Phadke, Y.D., *Politics and Language*, (Himalaya Publishing House, Bombay, March 1979, p. 8).
6. *Quoted in* Pendse Lalji, *Maharashtrache Mahamanthan-* (Lokvangmay-gruha Prakashan, Mumbai, 2010, p. 21).
7. *'Gandhi's thoughts on linguistic provinces'* compiled by Bharatratna Kumarappa July 1954. Gandhi was of the opinion that linguistic reorganisation has to be done without further delay. However, he was not in favour of appointing a commission to decide on the boundaries of the state because he thought that the idea was foreign.
8. Austin, Granville, *Indian Constitution, the cornerstone of nation* 1966, OUP, New Delhi, footnote on page 241).
9. *Constituent assembly of India, (legislative)* 27th November 1947, pp. 793-796.
10. Phadke, Y D, *Visavya Shtakatil Maharashtra,* Vol.8, (Mauj Prakashan, Mumbai, 2007, p. 351).
11. Phadke, Y.D., *Politics and Language* (Himalaya Publishing House, Bombay, March 1979, p. 12).
12. *Ibid*, p. 13.

13. Talwalkar, Govind, *Yashwantrao : Vyaktitva ani Kartrutva,* (Yashwantrao Chavan Pratishthan, Mumbai, April 2012, p. 73).
14. Pendse Lalji, *Maharashtrache Mahamanthan-* (Lokvangmaygruha Prakashan, Mumbai, 2010, p. 3).
15. Potdar, Datto Waman- *Shroteho* (A collection of speeches by Datto Waman Potdar), (Venus Book stall, Pune,1959, pp. 57-87).
16. *Ibid*, p. 3.
17. Phadke Y.D., *Politics and Language*, (Himalaya Publishing House, Bombay, March 1979, p. 69).
18. *Ibid*, p. 4.
19. Detailed account of these developments can be found in Deo, Shankarrao- *Daiva Dete Pan Karma Nete* (Saswad Ashram Vishwasta Mandal Publication, Pune 1976).
20. Chausalkar, Ashok- *Comrade Shreepad Amrut Dange*, (Comrade Govind Pansare Amrut Mahotsav Samiti Prakashan, Kolhapur, May 2011, pp. 290-292).
21. Pendse, Lalji, *Maharashtrache Mahamanthan-* Lokvangmaygruha Prakashan, Mumbai, 2010, p. 332.
22. Pages 116-120 of the report of SRC quoted in Phadke Y D, *Visavya Shtakatil Maharashtra* Vol. 7, (Mauj Prakashan, Mumbai, 2007, p. 150).
23. Phadke, Y D, *Visavya Shtakatil Maharashtra, Vol. 7*, (Mauj Prakashan, Mumbai, 2007, p. 216).
24. Pendse, Lalji- *Maharashtrache Mahamanthan-* Lokvangmaygruha Prakashan, Mumbai, 2010, p. 88-89.
25. The full text of the memorandum titled Maharashtra as a linguistic province can be found at http://www.ambedkar.org/ambcd/03.% 20 Maharashtra%20as%20a%20Linguistic%20Province.htm
26. The full text of his book Thoughts on linguistic states can be found at http://www.ambedkar.org/ambcd/05A.%20Thoughts%20on%20Linguistic%20States%20Part%20I.htm
27. Talwalkar, Govind, *Yashwantrao : Vyaktitva ani Kartrutva,* Yashwantrao Chavan Pratishthan, Mumbai, April 2012, p. 109.
28. For a correspondence on this issue between Nath Pai and Nehru see Phadke Y D, *Visavya Shtakatil Maharashtra,* Vol. 8, (Mauj Prakashan, Mumbai, 2007, p. 319).
29. Phadke, Y D, *Visavya Shtakatil Maharashtra,* Vol. 6, Mauj Prakashan, Mumbai, 2007, p. 152.
30. *Ibid*, p. 152.
31. Bhalerao Nishikant (Ed), *Samagra Anant Bhàlerao,* Vol. I, 2nd edition, Darpan Pratishthan Nanded, July 2011, p. 320.

32. Pendse, Lalji, *Maharashtrache Mahamanthan,* (Lokvangmaygruha Prakashan, Mumbai, 2010, p. 2)
33. Phadke, Y D, *Visavya Shtakatil Maharashtra,* Vol. 7, Mauj Prakashan, Mumbai, 2007, pp. 99-100.
34. Ramrao Deshmukh, Gopalrao Khedkar, Aarti Patil, P K Deshmukh, Sheshrao Wankhede signed for Mahavidarbha. Bhausaheb Hire, Yashwantrao Chavan, Nanasaheb Kunte and Devakinandan Narayan signed on behalf of Western Maharashtra whereas Devisingh Chavan, Laxmanrao Ghatkar and MRs. Prabhavatidevi Jakatdar signed on behalf of Marathwada.
35. Pendse, Lalji, *Maharashtrache Mahamanthan-* Lokvangmaygruha Prakashan, Mumbai, 2010, p. 86.
36. Pendse, Lalji, *Maharashtrache Mahamanthan-* Lokvangmaygruha Prakashan, Mumbai, 2010, p. 104.
37. Kelkar Indumati, *Lohia,* (National Book Trust, 1983), p. 120.
38. Phadke, Y D, *Visavya Shtakatil Maharashtra,* Vol. 6, Mauj Prakashan, Mumbai, 2007, p. 173.
39. Pendse, Lalji- *Maharashtrache Mahamanthan-* Lokvangmaygruha Prakashan, Mumbai, 2010, p. 83.
40. Goa initially became union territory and later on an independent state. The struggle between Marathi and Konkani sucked the energies of two generations of Marathi and Konkani supporters. Konkani became the official language of Goa whereas Marathi became the associate official language. In reality however, the usage of Konkani remained on the periphery.
41. For details see Kelekar Ravindra, *Bhashik Sangharshache Samajshastra,* (Rajhans Prakashan, Panaji, 2008).
42. Pendse, Lalji, *Maharashtrache Mahamanthan-* Lokvangmaygruha Prakashan, Mumbai, 2010, pp. 381-383.
43. Mathkar, Jayanand, *Maharashtrache Shilpakar Barrister Nath Pai,* (Maharashtra Rajya Sahitya Sanskruti Mandal Prakashan, Mumbai, 2nd Edition, September 2008, p. 63).
44. See Pradhan, G. P. and Jadhav, R G (Ed.) *Nivadak Sadhana,* Vol. 1, (Sadhana Prakashan, Pune, 2007, p. 20) for this article by Sane Guruji.
45. Devgirikar Hire correspondence quoted in Phadke Y D, *Visavya Shtakatil Maharashtra,* Vol. 7, Mauj Prakashan, Mumbai, 2007, p. 83.
46. Pendse, Lalji- *Maharashtrache Mahamanthan-* Lokvangmaygruha Prakashan, Mumbai, 2010, p. 460.
47. For the infightings within the Samiti, see, Phadke Y D, *Visavya Shtakatil Maharashtra,* Vol. 8, Mauj Prakashan, Mumbai, 2007.
48. Pendse, Lalji- *Maharashtrache Mahamanthan-* Lokvangmaygruha Prakashan, Mumbai, 2010 p. 492.

49. Phadke, Y D, *Visavya Shtakatil Maharashtra,* Vol. 8, Mauj Prakashan, Mumbai, 2007, p. 351.
50. For the text of his speech see, Nondi- *Vidhimandalatil Nivadak Bhashane*- Maharashtra Vidhanbhavan amrutmahotsav Samiti, Mumbai, 2011, pp. 84-105.
51. Talwalkar, Govind, *Yashwantrao : Vyaktitva ani Kartrutva, Yashwantrao Chavan Pratishthan,* Mumbai, April *2012,* p. 98.
52. Pendse, Lalji, *Maharashtrache Mahamanthan*- Lokvangmaygruha Prakashan, Mumbai, 2010 pp. 330-332.
53. Bedekar, D.K., *Samyukta Maharashtra*, (Chitrashala Prakashan, Pune 1947), pp. 55-57.
54. Chausalkar, Ashok, *Comrade Shreepad Amrut Dange, Comrade Govind Pansare Amrut Mahotsav Samiti Prakashan,* Kolhapur, May 2011, pp. 284-285, 428.
55. Dange's speech titled 'Shivaji – Tyancha ani Aamcha' at Amar Hind Mandal Dadar on 3rd May 1959 reproduced in Dange S.A.- *Bara Bhashane*, Abhinav Prakashan, Mumbai, January 1967, pp. 110-117.
56. Adarkar, Neera and Menon, Meena, *Katha Mumbaichya Girangaochi*, (Mauj Prakashan, Mumbai, 2009).
57. Lele, R.K., *Marathi Vruttapatrancha Itihas,* (Continental Prakashan, Pune, Third edition), p. 691.

Chapter 4

Congress and Language Politics in Maharashtra

It is true that the Congress Party refrained from getting involved in the politics of identity including that of language. However, it is also true that it has been the Congress ruling party in Maharashtra for almost 45 years of the states existence. During this period, the party had to deal with the various issues pertaining to Marathi language, culture and Marathi speaking people.

Soon after the creation of the state of Maharashtra, the internal fissures within the Samyukta Maharashtra Samiti gradually went public. The Committee was a coalition of various political parties and groups in Maharashtra. The communists and socialists who had managed to stay together in the committee until then were now in disagreement over the continuation of the movement and its future agenda. Yashwantrao Chavan and the ruling Congress took this opportunity to break the Samiti. The Peasants and Workers Party leadership was wooed by the Congress arguing that Samyukta Maharashtra is a Maratha dominant state and therefore it would be prudent on their part to join the ruling alliance and share the spoils of power rather than relegating to the political margins by being in the opposition.[1] As it is, the Non-Congress Parties in Maharashtra had a weak organisational base. Despite the popularity of the Samyukta Maharashtra Samiti, the constituent parties of the Samiti were not able to expand their support bases. It appears that the Marathi people had looked at the Samiti as a political alternative to the Congress, when the movement was at its peak. However, the increasing bickering between the various factions of the Samyukta Maharashtra Samiti might have eventually frustrated them. Possibly, as a result, the Samiti suffered defeat in the 1962 General elections. Political power remained in the hands of the Congress Party, many of whose members had either opposed the creation of Maharashtra or failed to take a position due to the fear of the Congress High Command. It is in this context that this chapter attempts to evaluate the role of the various Governments in Maharashtra led by the Congress Party in language politics and policies of the state.

4.1 Chavan's Ideas and Initiatives about the Development of Marathi Language

After taking over the responsibility as the Chief Minister of Unified Maharashtra, Yashwantrao Chavan spelled out his vision about the development of the state and development of the Marathi language. He responded to the apprehensions about the new state becoming a Maratha state instead of a Marathi state due to the numerical dominance of the Maratha Caste. He assured everyone that as long as he is in power, he would not allow the state to be dominated by any single caste.[2] While expressing the need to run the administration of the state of Maharashtra in Marathi language instead of English, he cautioned that this change should not affect the efficiency of the administration. To promote this work, he proposed the formation of Directorate of Languages.[3] Chavan was aware of the fact that a language cannot develop unless it is used for the dissemination of advanced knowledge. Therefore, he strongly recommended the use of Marathi in higher education. He argued that education could not reach the lowest strata of the society unless it is given in regional languages. For him, use of Regional languages for higher education was a means of empowerment of the common people leading to the democratisation of our society.[4]

4.2 Establishment of Literary and Culture Associations

Immediately after the creation of the state, Chavan established following language, literature and culture related bodies.

- Bhasha Sanchalanalay. (Directorate of languages).
- Sahitya ani Sanskruti Mandal (Board for literature and Culture).
- Vishwakosh Nirmiti Mandal (Board for Marathi Encyclopedia).
- Vidyapeeth Grantha Nirmiti Mandal (Board for creation of university level reference books).

All these agencies were established under the General Administration Department, which was looked after by the Chief Minister himself.[5] These institutions were not really envisaged to be autonomous. Therefore, they became highly bureaucratised.

4.3 The Maharashtra Official Languages Act 1964

The Maharashtra Official Languages Act 1964 was passed in 1965. It states the official language policy of the state. The Act states that Marathi shall be the language of:

- The bills introduced (or amendments thereto to be moved) in either House of the Legislature of the State.
- In all acts passed by the legislature of the state and in all ordinances promulgated by the Governor of Maharashtra under Article 213 of the Constitution.
- In all orders, rules, regulations and by laws issued by the state government under the Constitution, or under any law made by the Parliament or the legislature of the state.

The responsibility to implement this as well as to enhance the use of Marathi in administration was entrusted with the Directorate of Languages by this Act.[6] The Directorate is expected to discharge the following functions.[7]

- To implement the Policy of the Government of Maharashtra on official language.

- To develop administrative terminology and advisory manuals.
- To develop scientific and technological terminology, and dictionaries for college level education.
- To develop legal terminology and make legal translations.
- To translate budgetary and other departmental rule books.
- To conduct training programmes and examinations in Marathi for Non-Marathi employees and officers of the Government of Maharashtra.
- To conducting Examinations for Hindi Language.
- To ensure the use of Three Language formula in the Central Government establishments in Maharashtra.
- To conduct Marathi typing and shorthand exams for English typists and stenos.
- To make translations in minority languages.

4.4 Implementation of the Official Language Policy

A Language Advisory Committee was established to aid and advice the government about the enhanced use of Marathi in the administration. Under the aegis of the Directorate, a number of specialised terminology dictionaries were published on subjects like Economics, Political Science, Biology, Physics, Commerce etc. Besides this, the Directorate published a number of books and dictionaries required for the effective functioning of the administration. Initially some of the dictionaries of the Directorate were criticised by members of the literary world. The criticism was majorly about the Sanskritized nature of the terminology, which the common people found unintelligible. The government argued that uniformity of terminology across Indian languages was one of the concerns while making the terminologies. The critics however argued that the terminology should be drawn from the various dialects of Marathi so that terms used by the people in day-to-day life can be used in terminologies.[8] To refute the criticism, the Directorate published a booklet wherein they justified coining new and somewhat unfamiliar words. They argued that precision and accuracy was of utmost importance as far as the coinage of terminology was concerned. The new terminology may sound difficult in the beginning, but with its continued use, people would eventually find it acceptable and easy. Over the years, the terminology is routinely used in government administration and people have more or less accepted it.[9]

Although the Directorate of Languages is authorised to inspect various government establishments for ensuring the use of Marathi, due to limited work force and lack of initiative, not much has been done in this regard.[10] The State Government made it mandatory for all non-Marathi gazetted officers to learn Marathi and pass a qualifying examination. Their increments were to be stopped in case they failed to comply with these conditions. It forced non-Marathi officers to learn Marathi and pass the required exam. The Directorate of Language has published two booklets- Compilations of rules and orders issued by the Government of Maharashtra for the effective implementation of the Maharashtra Official Languages Act 1964.The first volume includes rules and orders issued from 1965 to December 1987 and the supplementary volume includes rules and orders from January 1988 to July 1993.[11] The orders concerned with four related issues.

- Maharashtra Official Languages Act and Rules therein.
- Use of Marathi in the functioning of the State Government.
- Marathi and Hindi language examinations.
- Marathi typing/shorthand training and awards scheme.

Majority of the government orders are about increasing the use of Marathi in the functioning of the State Government. Most of the circulars are issued by the desk in the Directorate of Languages that looks after increasing the use of Marathi in state administration.

A resolution dated 16 May 1964[12] says that various forms of Bills which are preferred in the Treasury Offices can be filled in Marathi. The Directorate of language was given the task of translating English forms into Marathi. A series of circulars have been issued by the government urging its employees to increase the use of Marathi in administration. For example, a circular dated 1st September 1965[13] requests the employees that they should rigorously follow the government orders regarding enhanced use of Marathi. It is mandatory that the details of tours of Ministers and officers, nameplates and other boards in their offices should be in Marathi, the circular insists. All the departmental heads were instructed to personally look into these matters and ensure compliance. However, the circular was more of a request than an order.

A more stringent circular was issued on 29th October 1965.[14] It states in no uncertain terms that Marathi is the official language of government business by the Act of 1964 and therefore government employees will not be allowed to use any other language besides Marathi. The Circular mentions about Bhasha Vibhag (Language Department) that has published various relevant books to speed up the shift from English to Marathi.[15]

It also gives a detailed feasible work plan saying that every note writer should write notes on at least ten files in Marathi in a week. It also insists upon the uniformity of terminology across departments and makes it clear that there is no room for individual likes and dislikes and imagination. All departments have been asked to keep their employee register, movement register in Marathi. The circular requests the employees to be more proactive in this regard. The project of Marathikaran (i.e. running the government business in Marathi) can be successful only with the help of the support of the employees. In a letter to the Director of Government Printing Press written in 1966,[16] the deputy secretary of the General Administration Department says that a number of notifications are still issued in English. Original and Special forms are still published in English and this needs to be stopped at the earliest. It instructs the printing department to return the matter written in English and asks the concerned departments to get it done in Marathi for printing.

Thus, the government has taken many steps to ensure that its various departments comply with its orders on Marathikaran.

Unavailability of Marathi typewriters was cited as one of the reasons for inability to use Marathi in administration. A circular dated 31 May 1967 exposes this flaw.[17] It insists that a lot of business of the government, can be managed without typewriters, and therefore the excuse that typewriters are unavailable does not stand the scrutiny. It also states that Rubber stamps and seals routinely required for the administration must be in Marathi Feels like repetition.

As the Government of Maharashtra had begun to make rules for increasing the use of Marathi in administration, the Ministry of Home Affairs of the Union Government had also started encouraging increasing use of regional languages in administration. The MHA called for submitting bi-annual reports on usage of regional languages in administration. A circular dated 7th October 1968[18] reveals that the performance of the administration was unsatisfactory as far as the use of Marathi is concerned. This circular calls upon the various department heads to consider increasing the use of Marathi in administration as their departmental duty. It further suggests the implementation of a phased programme for this purpose.

Two circulars dated 6th August 1969 and 12th February 1970[19] deal with government advertisements that are published in English in Marathi newspapers. It states that a number of government advertisements in Marathi newspapers especially district level newspapers are still published in English. It instructs all departments to publish all the government advertisements in Marathi newspapers in Marathi.

In 1972, the government instructed all the ministerial departments to conduct their daily business in Marathi. A bi-annual report about the use of Marathi in different departments was to be sent to the Directorate of Language on 5th January and 5th July every year.[20] It is not clear whether this practice continues.

Going a step further, a circular dated 28th November 1973[21] states that the business of various government departments should be conducted first in Marathi and then translated into English rather than doing it vice versa. This circular also specifies that the responsibility of the Directorate of languages is restricted to translation of standard forms and departmental manuals. It was meant to prevent the practice of giving all translation work to the Directorate. Another circular dated 21st November 1974[22] claimed that the bi-annual reports submitted by various government departments about the usage of Marathi do not reflect reality. Therefore, the Director of language has been entrusted with the power of field inspections of various government departments. This was an important change. Until then the government believed that the departments have the ability as well as the willingness to increase the use of Marathi. By this time, however it had realised that the belief was misplaced and stringent measures were required.

4.5 Raj Bhasha Varsha and Subsequent Developments

There was a growing concern about the use of regional languages at the union government level. It was believed that greater use of regional languages in administration would enhance transparency as well as accountability. In order to address these pressing issues, the year 1979 was declared as Raj Bhasha Varsha (Official Languages Year). It was an attempt to boost the confidence of those who propagated enhanced role for regional languages in administration. The All India Raj Bhasha Conference reviewed the all India scenario and made various recommendations. The Government of Maharashtra issued a circular[23] to ensure that these recommendations reach to its bureaucracy. The recommendations were:

- Various enactments by the Central Government as well as respective state governments for the implementation of Official Language policies do not seem to be adequate. English is routinely used in transacting government business. This has to stop immediately.

- In a number of cases, documents are still translated from English to regional languages, thus making regional languages secondary and creating obstructions in their use. Therefore, it is imperative that government business should be originally transacted in regional languages in most of the cases.
- The administrative language should be lucid and easily intelligible for the common people as well as government employees.

One important fact that came out of these recommendations as revealed by the conference, is that the problems faced in the implementation of Marathi in Maharashtra are about the same as faced by other states while implementing their respective language policies. Languages are going through similar problems in their respective states. Thus, these problems have to be understood in a larger Indian context and solutions to these problems can be found at the all India level.

It has been discussed earlier that the bureaucracy was dragging its feet on the use of Marathi. However, a circular dated 22nd January 1979[24] mentions about a meeting of a high-powered committee headed by the chief minister. The Chief Minister (Sharad Pawar at that time) gave orders to the Cabinet ministers as well ministers of state that they should insist upon the use of Marathi and they themselves should use Marathi. The circular is important because it also exposes the unwillingness of ministers to work in Marathi. The circular in a way accepted that neither the bureaucracy nor the politicians were in a hurry to complete the task of use of Marathi in administration. Whether the orders of the Chief Minister were followed is not clear.

Another circular[25] appeals to the administration that maximising the use of Marathi in government functioning is in the interest of the common person and makes the government responsive to people's sentiments. It further says that in the period of transition from English to Marathi certain issues have to be handled more sensitively. The focus should not be on the purity of Marathi language. Even if the language is a mixture of English and Marathi, it should be accepted. It also suggests that certain English words like Engineer, Commissioner and Typist should be construed as Marathi words and can be used in departmental notings. English short forms of names of certain departments (for example, L& JD for department of Law and Judiciary) should be continued to be used. One strange fact emerges through this communiqué. Besides the Directorate, the Law and Judiciary Department was supposed to take initiative in drafting the bills originally in Marathi and put an end to the dependence on English drafting. However, it seems that the Law and Judiciary Department did not take its task seriously.

Another circular[26] says the business in government undertakings should also be in Marathi. The circular is in the form of a request to State Government undertakings. Thus, while expanding the area of operation for business in Marathi, the tone and tenor of government action in this regard remains the same. Request, persuasion, and appeal to the conscience of the concerned people, is the modus operandi. While the government wanted to run the business of government undertakings, Corporations in Marathi, the reality was strikingly different. It was found that advertisements by semi-government undertakings, government-controlled corporations and boards were still given in English. Therefore, a government resolution[27] instructs the concerned establishments to ensure that their advertisements are published in Marathi.

One of the recurrent themes in these circulars is conducting the departmental examinations of government employees and the language of such examinations. Year after year, these exams were conducted in English under the pretext that study material was not available in Marathi. It is very strange that books like manual of office procedure, secretariat instructions, handbook of training for ministerial staff, Bombay Civil Services rules part one and two were not translated despite repeated suggestions. Probably no one was really in a hurry or imaginative enough to get these things done as per schedule. The same circular gives a list of 17 books that are to be translated out of which eleven books belong to the General administration Department, five to the department of finance and one book belongs to the Department of Energy, Industry and Labour.[28]

As mentioned earlier, the Director of Directorate of Language was given the powers to inspect various government departments as to whether they complied with the government's decision of increasing the use of Marathi in administration. The field visits were quite disappointing as the circular dated 10th October 1980[29] clearly illustrates. It states that the head office in Mantralay corresponds with various local, subordinate offices in English and therefore even the local offices have to respond in English. This means that the higher bureaucracy continued to use English. The circular squarely puts the blame on higher bureaucracy and states that their indifference is causing obstructions in the process of Marathikaran.

4.6 Silver Jubilee of the State and Renewed Efforts

The Government of Maharashtra decided to conduct the entire business of the Government in Marathi by the year 1985–i.e. the silver jubilee year of the creation of Maharashtra. Realising that earlier attempts of scrutiny on the field had not achieved desired results, the government announced constituting of a vigilance squad[30] that will visit various government departments and survey their functioning. It is not clear however, whether these squads were actually established, what surveys they undertook and what was its outcome.

It was a circular in 1982 that first talked about making the training of Marathi typing mandatory to all typists and stenos working in English. The circular instructed various departments to appoint Marathi typists in adequate numbers and for the first time mildly threatened that the establishment officers will personally be held responsible for any kind of non-compliance in this regard and that such non-compliance would be taken note of in the confidential reports of the concerned employees.

Whether such steps were actually taken or even this circular turned out to be an empty threat is not clear. In another circular,[31] the higher bureaucracy is criticised for not being proactive in the use of Marathi. It says that they would have no moral right to ask their subordinates to use Marathi if they themselves are not using it. Therefore, the higher bureaucracy is told not to ask for English summary of Marathi documents presented before them. To ensure better performance and accountability as far as the increased use of Marathi is concerned, a detailed proforma was prepared to get monthly details of use of Marathi in quantitative and qualitative terms. A demi government letter[32] in 1984 mentions this procedural innovation to ensure better compliance. Again it is not clear whether this practice continues and if it does, then to what extent it was effective. It was expected that all ministerial departments would create a 'form regulation committee' to translate and simplify forms required for the department. However, these committees were non-functional in many cases and burden of work was again shifted to the Directorate of Language.

It has been mentioned earlier that the power to scrutinise various government offices for compliance of the official language policy was initially given to the Directorate of Language. However, the office of the Director was too weak to effectively do this job. One reason for this was the Director of Language was ranked too low in the hierarchy and thus was rarely taken seriously. To overcome this problem, the task of monitoring various departments was handed over to the office of the Divisional Commissioner. Assistant Directors of the Directorate of Language located in Navi Mumbai, Pune, Nagpur and Aurangabad were to work under divisional commissioners of different revenue regions. Government Resolution[33] was issued to give a detailed work plan in this regard. It states that the divisional commissioners would submit a quarterly report of the same. Realising that various departments were still not complying with its orders, the government decided to constitute department level squads.

4.7 Change in Approach

By 1985, i.e. the year by which the Government of Maharashtra had aimed to bring complete Marathikaran of administration, the government was rather frustrated. A Government Order of 1986[34] clarified that if any government employee/officer was found to be dilly-dallying on the use of Marathi in administration, he/she would be penalised. A four stage punitive action was mentioned by the estimates committee for the first time that included:

- Written warning.
- Taking note of non-compliance in the confidential report of the employee.
- Fixing of responsibility.
- Postponing increment or promotion by one year.

Thus, the government had finally decided to apply the stick against errant employees. The number of employees actually penalised is not clear.

As we saw earlier, the responsibility of inspecting government offices was initially given to the Directorate. Later on, it was handed over to the offices of Divisional Commissioners of various revenue divisions. However, by 1989, this procedure completed a whole circle and the responsibility was again handed back to the Directorate of Language. This was done because the work required specialised knowledge, which the office of the Divisional Commissioner did not really possess.

After a very long time, the Chief Minister of the state had personally taken a note of non-compliance. A circular[35] says that the Chief Minister was unhappy that proposals before the government were not being presented in Marathi. It further warned that henceforth proposals submitted in English would be sent back without consideration and the officer who prepared and submitted the proposal in English would be held responsible for the delay. The tendency to sign in English on proposals submitted in Marathi was also criticised and employees were told to avoid it.

4.8 Why it did not Work

This detailed review of government efforts makes certain things strikingly clear.

- The State Government had never set any deadline for transacting the entire business of the administration in Marathi. Although there is mention of the 1985 deadline, it was more notional than realistic.
- The political elite does not seem to be committed to running the business of the government in Marathi, this despite the fact that majority of the members of the legislature were from rural Maharashtra where Marathi was the lingua franca of the people.
- Except very late, there was no mention of any punitive action against errant bureaucrats. Thus, there was no fear of punishment to those who defaulted.
- The Congress leadership including Yashwantrao Chavan who was quite an influential politician of the state until the early 1980s has not publicly criticised the bureaucracy for non-compliance, which meant that no one was in a hurry to speed up the the use of Marathi in administration. Ravishankar Shukla, the Chief Minister of the erstwhile Central provinces had refused to sign on files where notes were written in English. Had a similar approach been applied by the political leadership a Maharashtra, the use of Marathi in administration would have been quite impressive.

The Congress Party lost power in 1995. The Shivsena-BJP alliance was in favour only for a period of four years. Post-1999 politics was strikingly different from the earlier Congress politics in the One Dominant party politics phase. Post-1999, the Congress-NCP's democratic alliance was in power. However, it was a coalition government where there were multiple centers of power and the power of all ministerial offices including that of the Chief Minister was seriously compromised due to the compulsions of coalition politics. The period after 1995 is discussed in subsequent chapters.

4.9 Sahitya Sanskruti Mandal (The Board for Literature and Culture)[36]

Coming back to other attempts of language planning and development, the state government established Sahitya Sanskruti Mandal (The Board for literature and culture) on 19th November 1960.[37] The functions of the board include the following:[38]

- To promote and financially support research schemes and projects in the fields of literature, culture and history of Maharashtra and to conduct such projects through the Board itself.
- To encourage the use of Marathi in such researches and to publish them under the aegis of the Board itself.
- To encourage the publication of independently written scholarly theses, monographs, books, periodicals and other writings in Marathi or publishing it through the board.
- To encourage the publication of encyclopedias, dictionaries (by external agencies) or publishing it through the board itself.
- To translate scholarly books (not already taken by the Sahitya Academy) from other Indian and foreign languages into Marathi.
- To edit and compile published or unpublished documents directly or indirectly useful for the understanding of Maharashtra's history and culture.
- To initiate schemes about editing and publication of social, political, cultural and literary history of Maharashtra.
- To undertake surveys in different disciplines for the enrichment of Marathi literature.
- To help the government to initiate a policy on historical research and enrichment of literature.

Eminent Thinker Tarkateertha Laxmanshastri Joshi who was close to Yashwantrao Chavan was the first Chairman of the Board. Presently, Baba Bhand (2015) is the Chairman of the Board. The board has a panel of advisors generally litterateurs who aid and advise in the functioning of the board. Some of the major activities of the board are:

- Publication of Books originally written in Marathi and translated Books. Till date the board has published 487 books and 17 dictionaries.
- From 1981, the board gives Gauravvrutti to two persons every year- one from the field of literature and the other from the cultural field.
- Grants and donations- Through the Board, the Government of Maharashtra gives assistance of rupees 25 lakhs every year for the Akhil Bhartiya Marathi Sahitya Sammelan. Besides this, seven literary organisations across Maharashtra are given five lakh rupees per year for the spread of literature. The Board also gives rupees 25,000 each to 44 periodicals.
- It gives grant to new writers so that they can publish their initial writings.
- It conducts workshops for new, upcoming writers.

Although reasonably good work has been done by the board, much more could have been done had the board been given sufficient funds and required manpower. However, like the Directorate of Language, the Board has also been on the margins of political attention. Until recently, the Board was looked after by the Department of Cultural Affairs, generally handled by successive Chief Ministers. Even when the portfolio was handled by a cabinet rank minister, successive chief ministers have paid attention to the Cultural Affairs Ministry because it gives them required publicity. Language related agencies seldom get the attention of the political leaders because they are generally perceived to be non-glamorous and monotonous. This perception has continued through the last

50 odd years. A number of ministers and senior politicians of the government were either not aware of the existence of these agencies; and those who were aware of it, did not know what was the impact of such functions. Thus, it is not surprising that the Sahitya Sanskruti Mandal was always weak on the manpower front. As of 2011, the board has six permanent employees. That shows the government's initiative on this issue.

4.10 Vishvakosh Nirmiti Mandal[39]

Besides the above two agencies Vishwakosh Nirmiti Mandal was a major venture initiated by Yashwantrao Chavan under the intellectual mentorship of Lakshmanshastri Joshi. Maharashtra has a glorious tradition of producing Dnyankosh or Encyclopedia under the stewardship of Shridhar Vyankatesh Ketkar. His intellect and entrepreneurial skill made it a major intellectual venture in modern Marathi. After the creation of Maharashtra, the state government took it upon itself to publish the Encyclopedia in as many as 20 volumes. Initially, the Vishvakosh Samiti (Committee for the preparation of encyclopedia) was part of the Sahitya Sanskruti Mandal with its head office in Wai- near Satara. Tarkateertha Laxmanshastri Joshi worked from Wai. It was believed that a quieter place like Wai would create conducive atmosphere for a major intellectual venture like Vishvakosh. The First set of volumes were published from in 1976. In the preface to the first volume, editor in Chief of the Vishwakosh project Tarkateertha Lakshmanshastri Joshi has explained in detail the challenges he and his team faced during the venture.[40] This preface is significant in many respects. It lays down the government's vision clearly that it wants to see Marathi as the language of modern, higher knowledge. It looks at the Vishvakosh as the vehicle to this end. More importantly, the editor also acknowledges the fact that merely publishing of the 20,000 pages of Vishvakosh in 20 odd volumes is not sufficient. What is necessary is to update the work on an annual basis and publish it in the form of supplementary volumes. He also acknowledges the fact that over the years, some material in the Vishvakosh may become redundant and revised edition of the Vishvakosh may be needed.[41]

Government of Maharashtra made these volumes available to common people at a very affordable rate (Rest. 75/ - for a volume of approximately 1000 pages). Despite this, the Vishvakosh did not become a happening event in the intellectual life of Maharashtra as much as it was expected to be. As long as Yashwantrao Chavan was at the centre of Maharashtra politics, his favourite projects like Vishvakosh did get government patronage. However, by the late 1970s this began to change. Further even if Tarkateertha Lakshmanshastri Joshi gave a leadership to the Vishvakosh project, it can be argued that his staying the helm of affairs for more than three decades did bring in stagnancy. Lakshmanshastri Joshi died in 1993. After his death, M.P. Rege, an eminent scholar on Philosophy became the President of Vishvakosh Nirmiti Mandal followed by R. G. Jadhav and then Shrikant Jichkar. Presently, Vijaya Waad is the president of the Mandal. Her appointment was severely criticised by scholars across Maharashtra. However, the government of Ashok Chavan did not pay attention to the criticism and extended her term for the second time. Over the years, the Vishvakosh project has become a subject of ridicule. As mentioned earlier, updating, revision of the earlier volumes is not paid enough attention. Like Sahitya Sanskruti Mandal, the Vishvakosh Nirmiti Mandal also has a permanent problem of work force and financial crunch. The Wai office of the Mandal is in complete shambles. The need of modern information technology has dawned upon the Mandal a bit late. It was decided to put the entire Vishwakosh on CD. Initially all the pages of the Vishvakosh were scanned to prepare a bulky CD. After a series of criticism against such decision, the committee headed by Vijaya Wad has now planned to convert all the volumes in Unicode so that the matter becomes searchable on search engines like Google. However, the whole process is so slow that putting all the volumes on the net through Unicode with the present content itself will take another decade leave aside revising the volumes. Many persons have suggested to the Government of Maharashtra that all these volumes should be put on Government of Maharashtra's official website and citizens be invited to make additions to the matter and make relevant suggestions. To ascertain the authenticity of the matter posted, the government can appoint a multidisciplinary editorial committee that will ascertain the veracity of the matter posted and publish it after moderation. This will be like Wikipedia in a different form. Various organisations had even volunteered to key in the data of the Vishvakosh as a gift to the Government of Maharashtra from its people on the occasion of the Golden Jubilee of the creation of Maharashtra. However, such requests were ignored.

4.11 Vidyapeeth Grantha Nirmiti Mandal

One of the objectives of the initial language policy of the Government of Maharashtra was to make Marathi the language of higher knowledge in all the disciplines of modern life and to ensure that it becomes the medium of instruction at the graduate and post graduate level. To this end, Vidyapeeth Grantha Nirmiti Mandal (Board for publishing University level texts) was established. Its objective was to create university level textbooks so that students and teachers get adequate reference material when Marathi becomes the medium of instruction at the graduate and post graduate level. Clause 5 (55) of the Maharashtra Universities Act 1994 says that it is a part of the power and duties of the University to promote by itself, or in cooperation with other Universities the study of Marathi and the use of Marathi as a medium of instruction, study, research and examination.[42] It was expected that this task could be accomplished through the Vidyapeeth Grantha Nirmiti Mandal. Meetings were held with Vice-chancellors of the Universities to draw a realistic plan of making Marathi the Medium of instruction at the graduate and postgraduate level. University of Pune, established with the explicit objective of development of Marathi language, was expected to be proactive on this issue. However, soon Universities started dragging their feet on setting up a deadline for making Marathi available as the medium of instruction. As the gap between English and Marathi medium widened and almost became unbridgeable, the position of the universities became more and more ambivalent. Like the use of Marathi in administration, even the goal of developing Marathi as a medium of instruction had neither a deadline nor punitive action against defaulters. Soon, the whole exercise of Vidyapeeth Grantha Nirmiti Mandal became futile exercise. Around 20 years back, it was closed down arbitrarily. This author has enquired with several government officials and senior members of the state legislature. No one could tell what happened to this body, why it was closed down and to which department did it belong to before its closure.

4.12 Rajya Marathi Vikas Sanstha[43]

Realising that the government's efforts of development of Marathi language were going nowhere, the state government decided to establish a premier language development agency suitably titled Rajya Marathi Vikas Sanstha (State Institute for the Development of Marathi) in 1993. The objectives of the Sanstha were as follows:

I. To undertake multipronged efforts for the development of Marathi as the language of daily usage, administration and advanced fields of knowledge.

II. To develop resources for enhancing the use of Marathi in the fields of agriculture, medicine, industry, trade, commerce, science, technology, media etc. Developing language based technologies for various domains of social life.

III. To undertake time bound linguistic surveys and prepare status reports.

IV. To undertake programmes to enhance the use of Marathi in government and semi-government undertakings in order to make the use of Marathi people oriented.

V. To develop terminologies for generation of new knowledge in Marathi.

VI. To make Marathi language inclusive and accommodative by building bridges between the language of the elites and the various dialects of the masses.

VII. To develop suitable computer and web based technologies for the enhanced use of Marathi in Information and communication technology.

VIII. To develop resources for the Non Maharashtrians staying in Maharashtra so that they get an opportunity to learn Marathi language and understand Marathi culture.

Eminent linguist Ashok Kelkar and others were part of the team that drafted the constitution of this organisation. It was expected to be functionally autonomous and treated as an apex academic body to plan for the development of Marathi in different domains of social life. The slogan of the institute is "Development of Marathi, Development of Maharashtra." For the first time after the creation of Maharashtra, development of Marathi was so closely linked with development of Maharashtra on an official platform. This was a delayed but welcome realisation. In order to keep this institute out of the purview of bureaucracy, it was constituted in the form of a society. Sharad Pawar, the then Chief Minister of Maharashtra took keen interest in the formation of this institution and insisted upon its autonomy.

Eminent writer Sarojini Vaidya was the first director of the Institute. The Constitution of the Society provides for the appointment of 50 people as staff for various functions that the society would undertake from time to time. Unfortunately, this quota was never used fully. Presently the Sanstha has 12 permanent and seven non-permanent employees. Using the provision of autonomy against the employees, they were not given salaries according to the fifth and sixth pay commission on time. As of today, arrears of 11 years are still pending with the government. Issues of pension, gratuity are still not resolved. The condition of the non-permanent employees is even worse. They are given lump sum salary and are not eligible for any pay commission. They were promised that they would be absorbed as permanent employees. That has not happened so far. This has brought the morale of the employees down. Like the offices of other language and literature related agencies, the office of the sanstha is also in bad shape. Paucity of funds and almost a defunct regulatory committee are part of its organisational life. Going further, the government had planned the merger of Rajya Marathi Vikas Sanstha with Sahitya Sanskruti Mandal claiming that both organisations are involved into publishing of books and therefore there is avoidable duplication in their work. No one has bothered to check what the functions of these two institutions are and how they are fundamentally different.

Around 70 members from the literary and other fields are on these bodies as advisors. However, except a few who criticised the government for taking a mindless decision others have maintained studied silence on this issue. Although sustained protest by civil society organisations has forced the government to change the decision, a striking feature of the Marathi elite that emerges from this discussion is that they would not mind sacrificing their conscience for awards, grants or membership of coveted state run literary bodies. This is evident from the way many of them have dissociated themselves from key language debates and consequent confrontation with the government or bureaucracy.

Throughout the last 51 years (of which Congress was in power for more than 40 years) language and literature related secretaries of the General Administration Department for whom these agencies were nothing less than an avoidable burden mostly ran these agencies. Even the Directorate of Language was run without a full time qualified director for almost a decade. All these years, a deputy secretary of the General Administration Department worked as in-charge Director. There was hardly any agenda worth discussing. After a sustained campaign by language activists, the Department of Marathi Language was established in 2010. It took one more year to appoint a full time secretary for the department. During a personal interaction at his residence, the then Chief Minister Ashok Chavan[44] had told that the department of Marathi being a very small department would not require a full time secretary. When it was brought to his notice that other states in India are running full-fledged language departments and making adequate financial provisions for it and looking at the backlog of language related issues in Maharashtra a full-fledged department is needed, he was non-committal.

4.13 Evaluation

A close overview of the functioning of Maharashtra Government's language and literary agencies gives us the feeling that the state is both inefficient and indifferent towards language related issues. The state government has paid notional tribute to its official language. Within the Congress leadership there seems to be a difference in approach. Those with grass root support and mass following like Yashwantrao Chavan, Vasantdada Patil, and Sharad Pawar have taken initiative in the development of Marathi. Chavan for example started most of the literary agencies; Vasantdada forced the business of many departments to be done in Marathi whereas Sharad Pawar worked on the idea of an autonomous Rajya Marathi Vikas Sanstha. Even if these efforts may not be sufficient, but these leaders deserve the credit for initiating certain processes.

4.14 Use of Marathi in Other Domains

Earlier in this chapter, we have discussed the government policies towards use of Marathi in administration. There are other domains of social life where the government policy has a direct or an indirect impact. Let us take few representative examples and find out how the Congress has performed.

- ***Use of Marathi in Judiciary***

Immediately after independence, there was a general agreement that the local judiciary i.e. district and taluka level courts should entirely function in the regional languages. Going further, the Constitution of India says that if the state legislature passes a unanimous resolution and if the President of India consents upon it, Official language of a state can become the authorised language of the High Court of that state. Using this provision, Hindi-speaking states of North India like Uttar Pradesh, Bihar, Madhya Pradesh and Rajasthan have declared Hindi as the official language of their respective High Courts. States like Tamil Nadu and West Bengal have passed a unanimous resolution to make Tamil and Bengali the authorised language of their respective high courts. Tamil Nadu government announced the allocation of 300 crore rupees for the infrastructure required for this transition from English to Tamil. Use of regional languages in local courts has become a reality in most of the states with states of Northern India, states of the south like Tamil Nadu and states in the western part of India like Gujarat taking the lead. Maharashtra is an exception. In fact, the decision to make Marathi the language of lower courts should have been taken along with the enactment of Maharashtra State Official Language Act in 1965. Leading lawyers and judges favoured this transition. However, the government did not do the needful until 1998. Until then no government showed any proactive interest as far use of Marathi in the lower judiciary was concerned. In 2005, the High Court of Mumbai issued a circular to the lower courts asking them to do at least 50 per cent of their business in Marathi. Even this target has not been achieved in many districts of Maharashtra as an RTI query reveals.[45] The usual excuses of inadequacy of computers, unavailability of funds and software are seen here as well. This has brought things to a standstill. Government of Maharashtra had issued a government resolution in 1997 which gave one year deadline by which all the laws would be drafted originally in Marathi rather than translating from English to Marathi which was the usual practice. Fourteen years have passed since then and laws are still drafted in English. In a meeting with Chief Minister Ashok Chavan and Deputy Chief Minister Chhagan Bhujbal, this issue was raised.[46] Both of them were unaware of any such G.R. by the government. When a copy of it was shown to them, they were non-committal. Thus, beyond the usual administrative set up as well the governments mostly headed by the Congress could not do much for the usage and promotion of Marathi.

- ***Marathi as a medium of instruction***

Marathi was the medium of instruction in majority of the schools in Maharashtra. Although there were private aided and unaided schools, majority of the children went to schools run by Zilla Parishads and municipal councils or corporations. Although the quality of teaching in these schools was generally above average, the condition of the buildings was generally not good. Gradually with the spread of education, the composition of the student as well as teaching community in these schools changed. People from the upper castes and middle, upper middle classes who used to send their children to government or private run Marathi medium schools changed allegiance and started sending their children to aided or unaided English medium schools. People from other castes and classes in the areas followed them. Now this trend has reached semi-urban areas and villages. With the arrival of CBSE, ICSE and other international boards, rich parents are spending huge amounts to send their children to these Schools. Most of these schools do not have Marathi even as second or third language. One may really ask what the state can do if people are sending their children to English Medium schools. It is generally found that parents send their children to English medium schools because they do not want their children to lag behind in English and be deprived of modern technology-things considered as key for advancement in modern life. Had the government ensured parents that even after studying in Marathi medium schools their children would not be deprived of English and Technology, sizeable number of people would have been assured and that would have definitely helped in reversing the trend. Besides that, the government could have brought to the notice of the people the advantages of education in mother tongue. Ironically, children of most of the bureaucrats, politicians (including those who publicly champion the cause of Marathi) go to English medium schools. This duplicity frustrates the common people even further. Most of the MLAs, MPs run English medium schools arguing that it is in the interest of the Bahujan Samaj. This has become one of the key aspects of negotiations in the era of coalition politics. When the political elites propagate the cause of English and make it a part of their business plan, others are bound to follow. If we look at the growth of unaided English schools across Maharashtra and those who started these schools, we will get a clearer picture of how the political elites are exploiting the policy level anarchy as far as the issue of medium of instruction is concerned. Although all parties are part of this problem, by its sheer control over power the Congress has played a major role in it.

- ***Connecting with Maharashtrians outside Maharashtra and using their resources, expertise for the betterment of Marathi language and Marathi speaking people***

There is no formal mechanism within the Government of Maharashtra to connect with Maharashtrians outside Maharashtra. Maharashtrians are staying in other parts of India as well as in other countries of the world. Especially in the USA, hundreds of Maharashtrian software specialists have migrated for better economic prospects. Their help could have been taken in developing localised software solutions for Marathi. Hardly any attempt has been undertaken in this regard. In 1988, the first Jagatik Marathi Parishad (World Marathi Convention) was held in Mumbai in order to bring Maharashtrians across the world on one platform and ensure that their expertise is used for the betterment of Marathi and Maharashtra. This event was initiated by the Government of Maharashtra. Kusumagraj alias V.V. Shirwadkar the famous poet of Maharashtra who was later awarded Dnyanpeeth for his exemplary literary contribution was the president of this Convention. In his speech, he lambasted the Government of Maharashtra for making Marathi a beggar standing in front of Mantralay (the headquarters of the Government of Maharashtra) and begging for recognition. Although his speech has been quoted repeatedly by language activists, it has hardly made any impact on the state government as its later policies reveal. Later conventions of the Jagatik Marathi Parishad have also become rituals and more of a tourism venture rather than making it a genuine language or linguistic community driven programme. Same is the case with Vishva Marathi Sahitya Sammelans (World Marathi Literary Conventions) organised by the Akhil Bhartiya Marathi Sahitya Mahamandal – the apex body of literary agencies in Maharashtra.

These Sammelans are used for fossilised issues on literary discussions. There are exceptions but they merely prove the rule. It has become a tourist event for the Marathi literati partially subsidised by the state. This nexus makes the resolution of language-related issues even more difficult.

4.15 Conclusion

It would be clear from the above-mentioned discussion that like many other state governments even Congress Governments initiated language and literature development policies as far as Marathi is concerned. However, at the end of the day they appeared to have failed on many counts. Let us summarise these failures and causes thereof:

- There was no thought given to institutionalised development of language. For 50 years after the creation of Samyukta Maharashtra, language development agencies were handled by the officers of the General Administration who had neither the interest nor the expertise to run such agencies. It was only in the Golden Jubilee year that the State Government was forced to constitute a separate Department for Marathi. That is still in shambles as no serious thought has been given to its structure and functions.
- There is a general confusion between development of literature and the development of language. This has been further compounded by litterateurs patronised by the government who in turn offer legitimacy to the political elites for their alleged culture and literary consciousness. This false consciousness is difficult to challenge.
- The politics of the Congress was essentially caste-based and dependent on the party's hold on the rural areas. The problems of migration and consequent language and identity issues were less prevalent in the rural areas. Thus, the Congress did not identify with this form of identity politics. Emphasis on language politics would have made it difficult for them to forge caste alliances that they did so

successfully. Besides that majority of the Congressmen had never experienced the pain of fighting for a unilingual state. Thus, the language discourse was basically alien to them.

Against this backdrop, it is not difficult to gauge the language neutral responses of the Congress. How other political parties dealt with these issues would be discussed in the next chapter. Together that will give us a complete picture of the politics of Marathi language and politics of the Marathi speaking people.

Notes and References

1. For a detailed discussion of defections to the Congress from parties like PWP and the logic behind that see Talwalkar, Govind, *Yashwantrao : Vyaktitva ani Kartrutva,* Yashwantrao Chavan Pratishthan, Mumbai, April 2012, pp. 132-133.

   It is in this context that G. T. Madkholkar publicly asked Yashwantrao Chavan whether unified Maharashtra would be a Marathi state or a Maratha state. Although Chavan stated that it would be a Marathi state, later developments and Chavan's own grand design of the Maratha alliance reveal that Chavan aimed at a symbolically Marathi and practically Maratha state.
2. Maharashtrachya Bhavitavyachi Safar- Yashwantrao Chavan's speech at Sangli on 5th January, 1960 reproduced in Chavan Yashwantrao- *Sahyadriche Ware, Mukhyamantri Yashwantrao Chavan Yanchya Nivdak Bhashnancha Sangraha*- (Yashwantrao Chavan Pratishthan Mumbai, Third Edition, 1992), pp. 1-13.
3. *Ibid.* pp. 56-57, *Nave Rajya*- Chavan's speech at the Bombay secretariat during the oath taking ceremony of the Government of Maharashtra's new cabinet. This cautious approach has come in the way of speedy Marathikaran of the administration.
4. Yashwantrao Chavan's speech at the foundation stone laying ceremony of K. J. Somaiya Arts and Commerce College on 7.9.67 at Kopargaon Reproduced in *Yugantar- Chavan Yashwantrao, Nivdak Bhashane*, Continental Prakashan, Pune, 30, Third Edition, 2006, pp. 169-176.
5. The practice of keeping all these agencies under the not so related General Administration Department continued until 2010 and is one of the major reasons for the Government inaction on this issue.
6. The details about the Directorate of language can be found at http://bhasha. maharashtra. gov. in
7. http://www. gms. maharashtra. gov. in/bhasha/PrashasanikLekhanKosh. aspx

8. The details of various aspects of the debate over terminologies can be seen in Shasanvyavaharat Marathi: Samasya, Swarup, Prakriya, Bhasha Sanchalanalay, Maharashtra Shasan, (year of publication not given), p1. 56.
9. *Ibid*, pp. 85-121.
10. The Directorate has a team of translators who are generally engaged in budgetary translations as well as translations of various government departments' reports. It is a routine practice in Maharashtra administration to pass on all translation work to the Directorate even if it can v\be easily done by the concerned departments. For almost ten years, the Directorate did not have a full time qualified director and the officers of the general administration department that controlled the directorate took additional charge of the directorate without really paying much attention to it. There are vacancies of assistant and deputy directors, translators; the language advisory committee is not in place. Retired Justice Narendra Chapalgaonkar who headed the Bhasha Sallagar Samiti (Language advisory committee) resigned in protest. Presently the Bhasha Sanchalanalay is headed by bureaucrats with little or no expertise in language development, thus making the organisation rudderless.
11. These two booklets are: (a) Maharashtra Rajbhasha adhiniyam, 1964 wa tyakhalil niyam ani adesh ityadinchya sankalanachi pustika (compilation of rules upto December 1987), Shasakiy Madhyavarti Mudranalay, Mumbai 1988, (b) Maharashtra Rajbhasha Adhiniyam, 1964 wa tyakhalil niyam ani adesh ityadinchya sankalanachi puravani pustika (compilation of rules from Jan. 1988 to July 1993), Shasakiy Madhyavarti Mudranalay, Mumbai 1996.

    It means that the Government has not compiled rules and orders from Aug. 1993 until 2011.
12. Resolution no. MIB-1064-M, dated 16th May 1964, quoted in Maharashtra Raj Bhasha Adhiniyam 1964 wa tyakhalil niyam, adesh ityadinchya sankalanachi pustika (A compilation of Maharashtra Official language Act 1964 and rules, orders issued therein) Bhasha Sanchalanalay (Directorate of languages), Mumbai, 1988.
13. Circular no. mabhava-1065-m, dated 1st September 1965, *ibid*, p. 18.
14. Circular no. mabhava- 1165-m, dated 29th October 1965, *ibid*, p. 18.
15. However, this Bhasha Vibhag seems to be a part of the Department of General Administration as no separate department of Marathi language was established within the Government of Maharashtra until 2010..
16. No. mabhava-1066-33670-m dated 8th September 1966 *ibid*, p. 19.
17. Circular number mabhava-1067/707-m, dated 31st May 1967, *ibid*, p. 20.
18. Circular no. mabhava 1068-37070-m, dated 7th October 1968, *ibid*. p. 22.
19. Circular no. MABHAVA-1069-M Dated 6th August 1969 and Circular no. MABHAVA-1069/84211-M Dated 12the February 1970 ibid, p. 23.

20. Circular no. MABHAVA-1072/M Dated 18th November 1972. *ibid*, p. 25.
21. Circular no. MABHAVA-1972-M Dated 28th November 1973, p. 25.
22. Circular no. Mabhava -1074-m, 21st November 1974, *ibid*, p. 26.
23. Circular no. mabhava. 1178/5703(1, 6. 14)28, dated 4th December 1978, *ibid*, p. 31.
24. Circular no. mabhava-1079/28 dated 22nd January 1979, *ibid*, p. 32.
25. Circular no. mabhava-1079/28, dated 29th June 1979, *ibid*, p. 34.
26. Circular no. mabhava-1079/28, dated 23rd July 1979, *ibid*, p. 34.
27. Government Resolution no. rabhava-1079/28, dated 5th November 1979, *ibid*, p. 36.
28. These details make the whole thing look like a dark comedy. One section of the department of General Administration is insisting upon the increased use of Marathi in administration whereas other section of the same department is delaying translation of important books that would facilitate the use of Marathi. Both the sections are handled by the same secretary and the same minister- generally the Chief Minister himself. Thus, it is evident that by creating a small segment for the promotion of Marathi within the general administration department, the rulers cleared their conscience and now they can defend themselves citing the inertia of the bureaucracy.
29. Circular no. mabhava-1080/2533/28, dated 10th October1980, *ibid*, p. 40.
30. Circular no. mabhava-1082/1690/64/20, dated 4th July 1981, *ibid*, p. 40.
31. Circular no. mabhava-1083/1358/20, dated 28th December 1983, *ibid*, p. 43.
32. Demi government letter no. mabhava -1084/ pr. 112/ 20, dated 3rd April 1984, *ibid*, p. 44.
33. Government Resolution no. Mabhava-1084-pr-271/20, dated 20th August 1984.
34. Government Resolution, GAD, no. mabhava-1086/434/pr. 161/ 86/20-b, dated 18th July 1986.
35. No. miscellaneous-1091/778/19, dated 2nd February 1991.
36. The details about the Sahitya Sanskruti Mandal can be found at http:// mahasahityasanskruti. maharashtra. gov. in
37. *Maharashtra Rajya Sahitya Ani Sanskruti Mandal: Sadhan ani Sadhya* - Maharashtra Rajya Sahitya Ani Sanskruti Mandal Prakashan, October 2010, p. 1.
38. The functions of the Sahitya Sanskruti Mandal can be found at http:// mahasahityasanskruti. maharashtra. gov. in
39. The details about the Vishvakosh Nirmiti Mandal can be found at http:// vishwakosh. org. in
40. Preface to the *Marathi encyclopedia : Marathi Vishvakosh- Khanda 1* pp. 13-18.

41. This preface was written on 14th May 1975. 36 years after that the Government of Maharashtra has not been able to complete even the first edition of 20 volumes that were proposed, leave aside updating, revision and publication of supporting volumes. That speaks a lot about the Governments proactiveness and initiative.
42. Principal, Kadam Dr Shivajirao S. and others, *Maharashtra Universities Act 1994*, Hind Law House 2001, p. 91.
43. The details about the Rajya Marathi Vikas Sanstha (State Institute for the Development of Marathi can be found at http://rmvs. maharashtra. gov. in
44. Meeting with Chief Minister Ashok Chavan in June 2010 at his official residence Varsha along with the members of the Observer Research Foundation to discuss the publication of a booklet on Information and Communication technology and Marathi.
45. In the Vidarbha revenue region, average percentage of Marathi judgments is 40. 58, For Marathwada it is 22. 1, for North Maharashtra it is 31. 4, for western Maharashtra it is 35. 94, for Konkan region it is 56. 72 and for Mumbai region it is 11. Quoted in Nyayachya Pratikshet Marathi – Adv. Santosh Agre, Marathi Abhyas Kendra publication 2010, pp. 48-50.
46. Meeting of language activists and media activists presided over by Chief Minister of Maharashtra Ashok Chavan, Vidhan Bhavan Mumbai 19th April 2010.

Chapter 5

Shivsena, MNS and Other Non Congress Parties

This chapter looks at the role played by various Non Congress political parties in case of issues of Marathi language, culture and the Marathi speaking people. That includes Shivsena, BJP (erstwhile Janasangha), Socialist and Leftist parties, various factions of the RPI and the Maharashtra Navnirman Sena (MNS). The focus will be more on the Shivsena and MNS because their politics relates directly to these issues. For other political parties language issues are not a part of their core agenda.

5.1 Emergence of Shivsena

Shivsena was formed in 1966 by Bal Thackeray and some of his associates to fight against the perceived injustice against the Marathi speaking people in Maharashtra especially in the city of Bombay. The emergence of Shivsena was not a sudden development. The declining importance of Maharashtrians in the political economy of the city of Mumbai was a matter of serious concern much before the arrival of Shivsena. Maharashtrians were the single largest community in Mumbai, but they did not enjoy superior status in many domains of social life especially economic life. Migration of people and consequent grabbing of economic opportunities was an important cause behind the unrest among the Marathi youth.[1] During the struggle for Samyukta Maharashtra, communist leaders like

Lalji Pendse had warned that it would be dangerous to overlook the economic problems faced by the educated middle class Maharashtrians.[2] However, in the charged atmosphere of the movement such an advise was not paid due attention.

Shivsena's initial targets were South Indians, especially Tamils and Malayalese, who they thought were taking away the clerical and officer level jobs from Maharashtrians. Curiously, Shivsena decided not to take on the economically entrenched Gujaratis despite the fact that the Samyukta Maharashtra movement had created lot of bitterness between Marathi and Gujarati speaking people. For Shivsena, *Marathi Manoos* was more of an instrument of politics, so was Marathi language. It did not aim at creation of capital that can be owned by the *Marathi Manoos* or challenging the hegemony of capitalist class (which was essentially non-Marathi). Had that been the case, the nature of Shivsena's politics could have been fundamentally altered.

Bal Thackeray started a weekly magazine called 'Marmik' prior to the establishment of the Shivsena. Marathi was not the initial agenda of the magazine. However, gradually it shifted focus to the Marathi cause. Through telephone directories and other sources, Thackeray and his colleagues prepared a list of non-Maharashtrians occupying higher positions in Government and Private Sector. These lists were periodically published in Marmik with the title "Vacha Ani Thand Basa" and subsequently "Vacha Ani Jage Wha." (Read and do not do anything about it, Read and do something about it).[3] The purpose was to bring to the fore the marginalisation of the Marathi speaking people in these areas. This created a channel for the urban educated middle class Maharashtrians to vent their anger against the unfavourable economic arrangement in the city. Thackeray organised a huge meeting at Shivaji Park on 30th October 1966, the success of which emboldened him. Attacks on the hotels owned by South Indians and other establishments started when the government looked the other way.[4]

On 21 July 1967, Shivsena organised a Morcha on Mantralay (the headquarter of the Government of Maharashtra) and submitted a memorandum to the Government.[5] It included the following things:

- Like other states, even in Maharashtra 80 per cent jobs should be reserved for Maharashtrians. Government of Maharashtra should implement a firm and strong policy in this regard.
- Employment exchanges across the state have employment registration cards of people desirous of getting the jobs. These cards should explicitly include details like- for how many years has the person been staying staying in Maharashtra, details of his/her education from KG to PG, the place of permanent residence of their parents, details of his/her mother tongue, whether he/she can speak, read and write Marathi etc. Recruiting authorities in the Government, Semi Government sector should be given instructions that other qualifications being equal, Maharashtrian cardholders should be given preference in employment.
- The officers of Employment exchanges should be Marathi only.
- There should be a record of people who come to Mumbai, greater Mumbai and other parts of the state. It should include details like – which state they belong to, where are they employed, where do they reside, what work they are involved in etc. If need be a separate office manned by few supervisors should be constituted for it.
- No factory or industry should be permitted unless it makes arrangement for residence of its employees. While giving license to factory or industry, the condition of 80 per cent employment to Maharashtrians should be rigorously implemented. In shops or flats constructed by the Housing Board or the Public Works Department of the Government, Maharashtrians should be given preference as tenants. Non-Maharashtrians who have usurped these shops or flats

should be removed and Maharashtrians should be allotted these shops or flats as per their number in the registration list. Officers in the Housing Board should be Marathi only.

- Personnel officers, managers in private enterprises should not be appointed without the permission of the state government. These personnel officers should submit a quarterly report to the government about new appointments and departments where these appointments were made, details of transfers, terminations and reasons thereof, details about the percentage of Maharashtrians among the employees and officers in different classes and whether the number fulfills the condition (that 80 per cent employees should be Maharashtrians). If the required information is not given or if the information given is proved wrong, the state government should have the right to sack the recruiting officer of the concerned establishment.
- While appointing senior officers in Zilla Parishads, Municipal Corporations, District police headquarters, Maharashtra State Electricity Board, Housing Board, and Agriculture related departments, care should be taken to ensure that they could fluently read, write and speak Marathi. Presently there are no stringent guidelines in this regard.
- The functioning of Departments like Railways, Post, Telegraph, Telephone, Insurance Corporations, and Central Government Projects (that are operational in Maharashtra) should be in Marathi as they come directly in contact with the people of Maharashtra.
- Educational and cultural organisations run by Marathi speaking people in other states of India should be given economic assistance based on their need and performance. Institutions run by Non-Maharashtrians in the state should be given such assistance only on reciprocal basis. For example, Organisations run by Gujaratis should be given assistance only if the Gujarat Government is giving assistance to Marathi organisations in Gujarat.

- Three New centers of the All India Radio should be created-one each for Marathwada, South Maharashtra and North Maharashtra. Demand should also be made to enhance the transmission capacity of All India Radio Centers in Pune, Nagpur and Goa.
- Provision should be made for a big port like Kandla for the Konkan Region and a railway route that connects major cities. This should be provided for in the next five-year plan.
- Separate Universities should be established for Konkan and North Maharashtra.
- Geological Survey of Konkan and Vidarbha should be immediately undertaken to explore the availability of minerals.
- Deserving Maharashtrian scientists, technicians, mechanics, and researchers should be located and they should be given long-term loans individually or collectively. This should be done in order to ensure the spread of industry across Maharashtra.
- The state and the municipal corporations should not help outsiders in slums in getting alternate accommodation. Migrant beggars, outcaste criminals and unemployed should be immediately expelled from the state.
- Maharashtrians displaced due to town planning measures should not be displaced without giving alternate accommodation.
- Theatres should be immediately made available for Marathi films. Studios should be built for the production of Marathi Cinema.
- Government, semi-government and other employment should be given only to those who can write and speak Marathi fluently. This should be applicable especially to Doctors and Nurses.
- The present education system should be drastically revised keeping in mind that Marathi youth are lagging behind in

English. Liberal marking scheme should be implemented in S.S.C. and other exams keeping in mind the practices adopted by other states.

- All Government, Non-Government programmes or programmes by educational Institutions should begin with Maharashtra Geet.

5.2 Shivsena's Demands and the Response of the State Government

Shivsena appealed to the State Government that 80 per cent of the jobs in government and private sector should be reserved for Maharashtrians. The government accepted the demand. In 1973, Government of Maharashtra brought a resolution and made amendments to the Factory Act. However, the biggest issue was the definition of Maharashtrians. The initial definition was based on mother tongue of the person. One whose mother tongue is Marathi was considered as a Maharashtrian. The real difficulty for Maharashtrians in getting jobs was the way government defined a Marathi person. Officially, anybody staying in Maharashtra for a period of 15 years was called Marathi. Whereas Shivsena took the position that 80 per cent jobs should be reserved for those, whose mother tongue is Marathi. (This is similar to what Raj Thackeray is saying now. Now Shivsena has changed its position)

5.3 Who is Marathi? The Idea of the Domicile

On 2 March 1973, Manohar Joshi brought a private member's bill, which said that a separate department should be created under the Chief Minister titled 'Department of employment for locals'[6] However, due to the pressure of the industrialists the Government of Maharashtra expanded the definition of Marathi speaking person to mean domicile of Maharashtra i.e. that person who has stayed in the state of Maharashtra for more than 15 years. The industrialists were demanding for a change in the definition of the local or Bhumiputra that included the principle of domicile and language citing that the labour should have free access to move across the country for employment. On 15 February 1974, Minister of State for Home Affairs Kalyanrao Patil told the legislative Council members that it is not an order but just a recommendation of the government that employment should be given to locals. Government issued a new circular, which said that 80 per cent employment in the non-Managerial segment and 50 per cent employment in the Managerial segment should be given to 'locals'.[7]

The 'anti' component of the ideology was very strong. They were anti-South Indians, anti-communist and anti-Muslim. The focus was on improving the employment scenario for urban educated middle class Maharashtrians as discussed earlier. After the intervention of Shivsena, the number of Maharashtrians in the government and private sector went up, but Mary Fainsod Katzenstein says that it cannot be entirely attributed to Shivsena because the number of jobs had itself gone up. However, the resistance of the capitalist class had considerably declined after Shivsena's aggressive postures.[8]

5.4 Shivsena and its Allied Organisations

Besides the issue of employment to Marathi youth Shivsena has undertaken various activities through which it tried to mobilise the Marathi Manoos and became a political force to reckon with. Some of the allied wings of the Shivsena are listed below.

1. Bharatiya Kamgar Sena 9th August 1967
2. Bharatiya Vidyarthi Sena 10th August 1969
3. Bhadekaru Sena-15 August 1969
4. Chitrapat Sena-8 March 1970
5. Sthaniya Lokadhikar Samiti 1973
6. Sthaniya Lokadhikar Samiti Mahasangh 1974
7. Suraksharakshak Kamgar Sena 1986
8. Shramik Sena 1987 (started by Ganesh Naik- provision of ambulances)
9. Shivsena Mahila Aghadi 1988

10. Shetkari Sanghatana 1988
11. Dopahar ka Saamana -1993
12. Maharashtra cable Sena -1993
13. Grahak Sanrakshan Kaksha 1993
14. Baal Sena 2001
15. Yuva Sena 2010

Programmes to be implemented by Sthaniya Lokadhikar Samiti Mahasangh[9] are listed below. That would give us an idea of the multipronged programmes undertaken by the Samiti.

(A) Regarding Recruitment and promotions

- Insisting that advertisements regarding all categories of recruitment should be given in at least two major Marathi dailies.
- Based on the order of 8th May 1969 by the Government of India, a representative of the Government of Maharashtra should be appointed on all the public sector undertakings/ corporations of Government of India. Sthaniya Lokadhikar Samiti should insist on this.
- Sthaniya Lokadhikar Samiti should insist that in case of Employment in the class Three and class four services advertisements should only be given in regional papers.
- In Central Government establishments, written tests are allowed in English and Hindi. Such tests should also be conducted in Marathi.
- As per the order of the Government of India dated 18th March 1988, recruitment rules of various establishments can be changed after every five years. Sthaniya Lokadhikar Samiti should insist on this.
- In certain cases, educational qualifications like first class or second class in graduation are asked for. As per the order of the Government of India dated 18th March 1988, it should be changed to graduation or post graduation.

- To make efforts for changing the Recruitment rules to suit the Marathi candidates. While doing this, the educational standards in Maharashtra should be taken into consideration.
- While scrutinising the forms of candidates from outside the state, it should be verified whether the said candidates have graduated from colleges and universities recognised by the University Grants Commission.
- As per the rules laid down by the Government of India, 10 per cent jobs in Class three services and 20 per cent jobs in class four services are reserved for ex-servicemen. Information about recruitment for such vacancies has to be given to all the 23 District Sainik Boards at least three months in advance. Sthaniya Lokadhikar Samiti should ensure that these rules are rigorously followed in their establishments.
- As per the rules of the Government of India, seats reserved for scheduled castes and scheduled tribes should be filled up by scheduled caste and scheduled tribe candidates from Maharashtra.
- Welfare officer, Labour officer, Personnel officer, Safety officer and medical officer in various establishments should have the knowledge of Marathi.
- Training programmes should be organised for Marathi candidates ahead of various recruitment drives.
- If the Sthaniya Lokadhikar Samiti has adequate funds, it should distribute at least 50 copies of Employment news free of cost to Marathi employees.
- Circulars regarding Recruitment sent by the Sthaniya Lokadhikar Samiti Mahasangh should be immediately cyclostyled and given to Marathi employees of various establishments.

(B) Respecting the Marathi Language

- Forms, applications printed in Hindi and English should also be in Marathi. The order should be like this: Marathi first, followed by Hindi and English.
- Efforts should be done to ensure that there is due representation of Marathi language in the House Magazine of the Establishment.
- Circulars for employees should be published in Marathi along with Hindi and English.

(C) Cultural Programmes

- Shivjayanti Utsav should be celebrated in all establishments.
- Quality publications in Marathi should be purchased for the libraries of various establishments.

Sthaniya Lokadhikar Samiti became the backbone of Shivsena. It not only helped the Marathi Manoos in getting employment, but also helped the Shivsena party during various elections. It was the constructive face of the Sena. Many critics of Shivsena have appreciated Sthaniya Lokadhikar Samiti for its fundamental work. Unfortunately, the Samiti did not anticipate the changes brought in by the information and communication technology revolution. Therefore, it seems to have taken a backseat seat 1990.[10]

5.5 Issues on the Shivsena's Agenda

Besides the employment of the Marathi Manoos, Shivsena undertook various emotive issues.

- ***Struggle for the disputed border areas of Belgaum, Karwar, Nipani and Bidar etc.***

On 27 January 1969, Shivsena organised a Satyagraha on this issue. Agitators tried to stop Deputy Prime Minister Morarji Desai's car. However, Morarji Desai refused to accept the petition. This led to violence and 69 people died in the consequent firing. Shivsena Pramukh Thackeray was arrested for inciting violence.

On 2nd March 1970, Shivsena organised Mumbai Bandh.[11] Seeing that the government was not paying attention to the genuine demands of the people of border areas, another bandh was organised on 18th December 1973. On the legislative front Shivsena members tried to raise this issue. However, due to their limited strength, they could not use these weapons as successfully as they could have with more strength in the legislature. Shivsena seems to be the only party in the opposition, which has constantly taken a stand on the border issue.

In 1986, this issue erupted again. Chhagan Bhujbal then leader of Shivsena led a Satyagraha against the compulsion of Kannada in the areas in Karnataka bordering Maharashtra. In 1987, leaders of all parties in Maharashtra including Shivsena suggested that opinion poll should be held in the border areas. The Chief Minister of Maharashtra said that Maharashtra would support this idea. Eventually, differences on strategy arose between S.M. Joshi the socialist leader and Thackeray when the latter suggested that the movement might turn violent if the genuine demands of the people of the border areas are not met. Basically, Bal Thackeray was of the opinion that an all out struggle is necessary to resolve the boundary dispute. He had an argument with S M Joshi on this issue. Consequently, Thackeray withdrew from the Samyukta Maharashtra Seema Samiti that was formed to handle the resolution of the border dispute.[12]

On 26 November 2004, S.M. Krishna – the former chief minister of Karnataka became the Governor of Maharashtra. He had taken an anti-Maharashtra position from time to time as the Chief Minister of Karnataka. Therefore, Shivsena opposed his appointment. Krishna assured the Shivsena leadership that as the Governor of Maharashtra he would vouch for the position taken by the Government of Maharashtra.[13] As the Governor of Maharashtra, while addressing the assembly, S M Krishna had to follow the official line of the government that the disputed area belongs to Maharashtra. Looking at the symbolic and often insignificant nature of the Governor's address to the Legislative Assembly, it appears that Shivsena's gesture could bear only symbolic results. In last few years Shivsena's agitational spirit has declined as far as this issue is concerned. Shivsena has continued its support to the movement. However, it missed a major opportunity to resolve this problem when the NDA Government led by the BJP of which Shivsena was an important ally came to power in 1996 and then in 1998. From 1995 to 1999, the Shivsena-BJP alliance was in power in Maharashtra as well. Had Shivsena used this opportunity to pressurise the BJP, the issue could have been resolved. But it chose not to press upon this issue seriously. The Mayor and Deputy Mayor of Belgaum Municipal Corporation participated in the Black Day programme on 1st November 2011 to protest against the unfair inclusion of the border areas in Karnataka. On 1st November 1956 the state of Karnataka was formed. Taking an offense to this, the state government in Karnataka dissolved the Belgaum Municipal Corporation in the 1st week of November 2011. In June 2012, the Bengaluru High Court struck down this decision.[14] However, the Karnataka government again dissolved the Belgaum Municipal Corporation citing less number of meetings as a reason. MNS chief Raj Thackeray had advised the leaders of the Maharashtra Ekikaran Samiti that they should stay in Karnataka when the issue of dissolution of the corporation was widely discussed. Shivsena reaffirmed its stand on the issue by demanding that the disputed area be made a Union Territory. The above description clearly establishes the fact that with all its limitations Shivsena was a trusted ally of the people of the border areas.

- ***Marathi signboards on shops and other establishments***

Shops and Establishment Rules of the Municipal Corporation stipulate that, boards of various establishments should be prominently displayed in Marathi. Shivsena's campaign for Marathi boards started in August 1974. Thackeray warned that if Shopkeepers do not display Marathi Boards, English Boards would be tarnished. When Shivsena actually started the campaign, shopkeepers were intimidated. In certain areas of the city boards of

Shops and Establishments were displayed in Marathi. Casual attitude of the municipal employees towards erring shopkeepers and absence of tough penalty allowed shopkeepers to flout the rules about use of Marathi. In 2009, Maharashtra Navnirman Sena started the same campaign again. This time Shivsena was the ruling party in the Municipal Corporation of Mumbai. Therefore, Shivsena suggested the speedy implementation of Shops and Establishment Rules. Ideally, Shivsena should have implemented this rule meticulously during its regime in the corporation. However, its failure to do so helped the MNS to show the limitations of Shivsena's brand of Nativist politics.

- ***Renaming the city of Bombay as Mumbai***

Shivsena has always maintained that the name of the city is Mumbai and not Bombay. Shivsena legislators raised this issue in the legislature. Its corporators also raised this issue in the Corporation. In 1975, the Municipal Corporation of Mumbai had sent a proposal to the Government of Maharashtra regarding changing the name of this city from Bombay to Mumbai. However, the Government of Maharashtra rejected the proposal citing lack of merit in it. Finally, the proposal was sent to the Central Government for consideration.[15] On 27 January 1986, Mayor of Mumbai, Chhagan Bhujbal inaugurated a board that changed the name of the city from Bombay to Mumbai.[16] On 4th May 1995, the cabinet of Maharashtra headed by Shivsena decided to change the name of the city from Bombay to Mumbai.[17]

- ***Use of Marathi in the business of the Government***

The previous chapter has documented the record of the Congress Government as far as the enhanced use of Marathi in administration is concerned. Being an opposition party and that too a minor one in the state legislature for much of its existence, Shivsena could not do much beyond raising issues.

5.6 Shivsena's Silence on Use of Marathi in Administration

Shivsena either did not understand the issue of use of Marathi in administration or did not find it important to act upon. Had the Shivsena taken up this issue, the government would have been forced to act faster on the issue of 100 per cent use of Marathi in administration. However, as the next chapter will discuss in detail, Shivsena did not find this issue as important as it found the employment of the Marathi Manoos in the clerical segments of the public and private sector. The reason may be that the Shivsena had close ties with the then Chief Minister Vasantrao Naik who encouraged Shivsena's venture of breaking the leftist trade unions in the industrial belt of Mumbai.[18] The workers who suffered because of the paralyzing of trade unions were primarily Maharashtrian. There might have been a tacit understanding between the government and the Shivsena as the Shivsena never actually challenged the government on this issue. Another possibility is that although a number of senior bureaucrats were Non-Maharashtrian and the linguistic composition of the senior bureaucracy did play a negative role in the implementation of language policy in this case, the middle and lower rung of the bureaucracy included a large number of Marathi speaking people. Had the Shivsena taken up this issue, they might have had to go against their own brethren. Whatever may be the reason, it is true that the ruling as well as opposition parties did not show much proactiveness on this issue.

When Shivsena came to power in the state, its Chief Minister Manohar Joshi decided on the following things to pursue this objective:[19]

1. All laws to be drafted in Marathi and translated in English if necessary.
2. Functioning of the judiciary in Marathi.

Within the limits of its political strength, Shivsena tried to pressurise the government about the use of Marathi. However, throughout its political life spanning 45 years, Shivsena has never attempted to prepare a strategic note or action plan about the enhanced use of Marathi in administration. Had the Shivsena been alert to the tools of legislative advocacy, it could have used these circulars to further pressurise the government.

To make Marathi the language of the state legislature, the government issued a notification.[20] This was done in order to effectively implement the Maharashtra Official Languages Act, 1964.

Use of Marathi in the Judiciary

As discussed in the previous chapter the judicial fraternity has been slow in responding to the demands of Marathikaran. When the Shivsena-BJP Government came to power in 1995, it started taking steps about making Marathi the language of lower courts. In 1998, the government issued a notification thereby amending the Criminal and Civil Procedure Code and making Marathi the language of lower courts.[21] By these changes Marathi was made mandatory for the lower Judiciary in Maharashtra. However; it did not pursue the matter with the High Court of Mumbai during its term in the office.[22] A related but substantive issue is making Marathi the authorised language of the High Court under Article 348 clause 2. States of North India like Uttar Pradesh, Madhya Pradesh, Bihar and Rajasthan have made Hindi the authorised language of their respective High Courts since 1969. States of Tamil Nadu and West Bengal have made adequate provisions of providing infrastructure and other Human Resources for making Tamil and Bengali the authorised languages of their respective High Courts. During the tenure of Shivsena-BJP Government, the matter was brought before the minister of law and judiciary who belonged to Shivsena. However, no steps were taken by the government (correspondence between Shantaram Datar and others, Bar Council of Maharashtra and Goa and the Ministry of Law and Judiciary Government of Maharashtra).[23] The lack of enthusiasm of the Shivsena on this issue forces one to conclude that Shivsena is unable to comprehend the complexity of the language issues as far as the use of Marathi in the lower judiciary is concerned.[24] The details of Shivsena's activism on various issues related to Marathi language, culture reveals that the party has primarily focused on anti-migrant politics and employment of the urban middle class Marathi youth. However, that was not their flagship agenda. While executing this agenda Shivsena felt the need of developing allied organisations. This could be explained as the organic growth of the party. It is not clear whether Shivsena and its leadership did not understand the core problem at all or whether they understood but decided not to go ahead on that path because it was more difficult to tread. This has put Shivsena in a perpetual dilemma. Shiv Sainiks talk about the protection of Marathi language wherever they are in power. Thackeray has exploited this issue for elections. However, the grandchildren from the Thackeray family and those from the families of the leaders and many Shiv Sainiks are in English medium, Convents or even International schools, thereby undermining the very ideology they are talking about. It is not difficult to see why it happened. Shivsena did not have a comprehensive ideology for the upliftment of the Maharashtrians. Therefore, they did all that gave them immediate visibility and recognition. However, they were reluctant to take on fundamental issues and then follow them in their individual life. All of them consciously chose English as the medium of instruction for their own children when in the same breath they talked about the preservation of Marathi language. This fundamental lack of clarity is one of the core failures of Shivsena.

Shivsena has controlled many municipal corporations in Maharashtra[25] and has also ruled the state with BJP for four years. Despite this, Shivsena has not been able to do much to make Marathi the language of local self-government administration, state administration or judicial administration. For example, despite its long stint of power in Brihanmumbai Municipal Corporation, Shivsena could not do much for making Marathi the language of the Corporation. It succeeded only in 2008. As the records of the municipal debates show, the initial focus was on translating English documents in Marathi wherever required. Even today, the party has not succeeded in providing technical and human resource inputs for making Marathi truly the language of administration. Thus, the decision remains symbolic in nature. It may give political mileage to Shivsena. However, it does not address the basic issue of lack of will power and insight in making Marathi the language of administration.[26]

5.7 The Hindutva Dilemma

Shivsena made a shift of emphasis from Marathi Manoos to Hindujan during the 1980s. There were obvious electoral compulsions for this shift. Shivsena was able to enter the interiors of Maharashtra with the help of Hindutva ideology. When Shivsena officially shifted to Hindutva for electoral benefits, it had to accommodate all non-Maharashtrians because of the ideological demands. Thus, post 1985 Shivsena has neither been truly Hindu nor truly Maharashtrian. However, in the absence of a parallel organisation that could expose these limitations, Shivsena still monopolised the Marathi agenda.

5.8 Maharashtra Navnirman Sena

MNS was formed in 2006 by Raj Thackeray. Its formation was a result of a struggle between Raj and Uddhav Thackeray over leadership and the subsequent breaking away of Raj from Shivsena. The flag of his party includes the green and the blue colour. This has been interpreted as his party's openness towards accommodating Dalits and Muslims in the MNS. The website of his party[27] gives details about its vision. Some excerpts below:

1. Maharashtra Navnirman Sena is committed to raising the status of Maharashtra State, its people and the Marathi language to resplendent glory.
2. Maharashtra Navnirman Sena is concerned about the State of Maharashtra and its cultural and material prosperity. It is committed to the development of the Marathi language and expanding its knowledge base. It will work to spread the knowledge about Maharashtra and expand its cultural boundaries.

3. Maharashtra Navnirman Sena will bring the people of Maharashtra together, irrespective of caste, religion, sect or class, under its flag, for the development of Maharashtra.
4. The interest of the *Marathi Manoos* is of prime importance to Maharashtra Navnirman Sena. We believe the *Marathi Manoos* to be the person living in the State and born to Marathi parents, or one, though of a different linguistic origin, born in Maharashtra, who speaks Marathi and loves Maharashtra.
5. Maharashtra Navnirman Sena will strive to remove all impediments, resolve all problems that obstruct the development of Maharashtra State and the *Marathi Manoos* and will engage at all levels with those power centres, sects or social groups having vested interests who come in the way of this development. It will work in a constructive way for this purpose, at the same time; it will not shy away from conflict wherever necessary. Maharashtra Navnirman Sena makes no distinction between constructive and conflicting ways and believes that both go hand in hand.
6. To give justice to the Marathi Manus, Maharashtra Navnirman Sena will do everything, for example, establishing a Marathi Language Academy, fighting with the anti-Marathi lobby, making Marathi a compulsory subject in all schools, insisting for Marathi name-boards on shops and establishments to broadening the knowledge base in Marathi. These activities, constructive as well as street-level campaigning will be pursued at the same time.
7. Maharashtra Navnirman Sena will strive to put the Marathi Manus in the forefront of every field, be it roads, railways, electricity, water, health, education, sports, women, labour, tribal development, home, law and order, agriculture, tourism, finance, trade, business, cooperative sector or Centre-State relations.
8. Maharashtra Navnirman Sena will fight to its last breath to eliminate the interference of the non-Marathi power brokers

from outside the State in the State's politics and social life thereby reinforcing the existence of Maharashtra for the *Marathi Manoos*.

9. Maharashtra Navnirman Sena will take the Maharashtra State and the *Marathi Manoos* to the apex of cultural and material glory that the whole world will envy. This is the dream of Maharashtra Navnirman Sena, and the party will leave no stone unturned to make this dream a reality.

The vision statement of the party is an important document to look into the mind of its leadership. The definition of Marathi Manoos includes even those people who are born in the state not to Marathi parents but who speak Marathi. Another interesting factor is the collaboration of constructive and street politics. Importantly, whether it is the Shivsena or the MNS, aggressive strategies and street level politics have been the hallmarks of their organisational growth. It is seen quite frequently, that the cadre of these parties gets impatient if the party leadership toes peaceful line on issues that are close to heart for the cadre.

5.9 Core Programmes

Following are some issues taken by MNS

1. *Control the political dominance of migrants and protect the opportunities of the Marathi Manoos*

The MNS website says, "Migration from other States to Maharashtra has increased many-fold in the last few years. These illegal, unemployed migrants are claiming employment opportunities available in the State while the *Marathi Manoos* is left unemployed and the farmers are forced to commit suicide.[28] The political powers are also conniving to bypass the Marathi Manus and forcibly place the migrants in his position, causing the decline of the Marathi language and Marathi culture. Maharashtra Navnirman Sena will thwart these efforts to give opportunities to outsiders at the cost of the Marathi person and ensure justice for the Marathi-speaking populace."

- Issue of huge migration from north India – One of the important campaigns of MNS was against the North Indian migrants to Maharashtra. It started with an attack on few taximen and others in the informal sector.
- A related issue was that of the north Indians being allowed to appear for Railway recruitment examinations from Maharashtra. Raj Thackeray had taken up this issue even before the formation of MNS. After the establishment of MNS, students attending these exams were attacked again.[29]
- MNS also took the issue of Taxi and autorikshaw permits arguing that 80 per cent of these permits should be given to Maharashtrians.

2. Insist on Marathi language and Marathi sign-boards everywhere

MNS website says, "A culture exists only on the basis of a language, and a community exists only on the basis of its culture. Therefore, we must protect the Marathi language to protect the Marathi Manus."[30] Marathi nameplates on shops and other establishments is an important aspect of MNS Agenda. In fact, the recent MNS campaign (as the one by Shivsena earlier) of Marathi boards forced many a shopkeepers to change the nameplates from English to Marathi. In his letter written to owners of various shops and establishments on 14th July 2008[31] Raj Thackeray says, "Marathi is the State language of the Maharashtra State. In addition, as per the Shops and Establishments Act, 1948, all shops and establishments in the State are legally bound to display their names and conduct their business in Marathi.

In addition, you use the State's resources when you do business in the State and create wealth for yourself. By not using the State's official language for your business and on your display boards, you are insulting the State of Maharashtra and all the Marathi people. You are holding the language of the State in contempt, and this is a grave crime. You have had every opportunity to correct yourself, ever since the State of Maharashtra came into existence on May 1, 1960. Now, the Maharashtra *Navnirman Sena* will give you a period of one month to do the needful. If, in this period, you fail to change the boards displaying the name of your establishment and make Marathi the language of doing business, the Maharashtra *Navnirman Sena* will ensure that the people of Maharashtra State teach you to speak Marathi in the distinctive Marathi way."

Similar issue was that of showing Marathi films in multiplexes during primetime. However, this rule is generally violated. In one of his speeches, Raj Thackeray warned multiplex owners that they should follow the rule or face consequences. MNS workers attacked a few multiplexes and Raj Thackeray organised a meeting of various stakeholders in Marathi cinema to discuss future strategies.[32]

3. Make teaching of Marathi language compulsory in all schools in Maharashtra

"For the development of the language, Marathi must be taught to all school children from the very beginning. How can a school in Maharashtra not teach the language of Maharashtra? Maharashtra Navnirman Sena insists that the Marathi language must be taught in all schools, whether they are public or private, rural or urban, whatever be its medium of instruction."[33]

Thus, the focus is on teaching Marathi and not teaching through Marathi as a medium.[34] In his letter to all heads of the institutions running private schools in Mumbai and across Maharashtra, he says, "Your school is located in Maharashtra, a State whose official language is Marathi. If Marathi is being taught in your school as a compulsory subject from Standard I to X (or in the corresponding Grades), then I heartily congratulate you. If this is not so, then it is serious issue and against the interest of the State of Maharashtra. Perhaps no one has alerted you until now, and that is why I wish to make you aware of this blunder through this letter. All that is created on the soils of Maharashtra is created with the help of the natural resources available to the State. Your institution too, uses these resources. The electricity, water and other resources used by your institution are a part of the share of Maharashtra State. In spite of this, when your institution has not made the official language of the State a compulsory part of the syllabus, then I have no choice but to campaign against your institution." He expects even the CBSE, ICSE or IGCSE schools to teach Marathi as a compulsory subject.

4. On the Disputed border areas

On the issue of disputed border areas between Maharashtra and Karnataka, he criticizes the fragmented leadership in the region. Recently when the leaders of the Maharashtra Ekikaran Samiti met him on the issue of dissolution of the Belgaon municipal corporation, he advised them to abide by the rules of Karnataka and rethink about joining Maharashtra. He was criticised by people of the disputed areas. His criticism about the factionalism within the Maharashtra Ekikaran Samiti is misplaced. This was the consensual opinion of the Maharashtra Ekikaran Samiti leaders when this author interacted with them on the current situation (in 2010 and 2011)[35] on the issue.

5.10 Other Parties in Maharashtra and their Perception of Language Politics

Besides the Sena and MNS other political parties in Maharashtra include the socialist Parties (PSP and SSP), Communist Parties (CPI and CPM), Peasants and Workers Party; Jan Sangh and BJP, and various factions of the RPI. The PSP and the CPI were part of the Samyukta Maharashtra Movement. However, they differed on the issue of continuation of the struggle after the creation of Maharashtra. Then onwards, except in case of the PDF government, socialists and communists have never had any share of power in the state. Jan Sangh was in power during the PDF government from 1978-1980. After 1985 the BJP joined hands with the Shivsena. Therefore, although it did not directly talk about the issues of Marathi Language, it did share the concerns raised by Shivsena as an alliance partner. The Scheduled Caste federation of Babasaheb Ambedkar had participated in the Samyukta Maharashtra Movement. However, after Ambedkar's death various factions of the RPI have not discussed issues of language in detail. Most of the times factions of the RPI are lesser important partners of the electoral alliance and their leaders are co-opted by major political parties. That could be one reason why these parties have not discussed such issues in great detail. The PWP was also a member of the Samyukta Maharashtra Movement. After the creation of Maharashtra, many Maratha leaders of the party went to the Congress responding to the appeal of Yashwantrao Chavan. Like the Socialist and the Communist parties the influence of PWP also is restricted to a few pockets in the state. It would be difficult to expect much from political parties on the margins of political life in Maharashtra to take up language issues beyond their strength in the legislature. N.D. Patil, the leader of the PWP is still the mentor of the Maharashtra Ekikaran Samiti that has undertaken a relentless struggle for the inclusion of Marathi speaking border areas occupied by the then Mysore and present Karnataka state. The approach to issues of language and culture in general and Marathi language and culture in particular of these parties have to be searched through their Election Manifestoes, legislative debates or related documents. An account of these parties' views related to language is given below. The discussion of manifestoes is not exhaustive but representative in nature. It will give us an idea of the views of parties other than Congress and Shivsena.[36]

The CPI(M) Election Manifesto of 1967[37] says, "The Congress Party has undertaken a mindless work of replacing English by Hindi rather than giving equal status to all Indian languages. This has jeopardised the unity and integrity of the country. When people opposed this in Tamil Nadu, the struggle was brutally suppressed. The Congress party is not interested in developing the languages of people and running the administration through them. The Congress does not assure that regional languages would become the medium of instruction until University level education. This has helped in continuation of the influence of English and regional languages relegated to the margins. Due to the arrogance of the supporters of

Hindi, people are resisting Hindi. That has encouraged the use of English."

Going further, the Party demanded that the citizens must have the right to get education through their mother tongue. Interestingly, it mentions the regional languages as the National languages of different nationalities. The underlined assumption is that various linguistic groups are nationalities and language is the defining character of that identity. An interesting feature of the Manifesto is the demand for simultaneous transition from English to Hindi at the National level and from English to regional languages at the state level. The Manifesto demands that all national languages would be treated equally in the Lok Sabha and the Central Government. All members should have the freedom to speak in any national language (included in the Eighth Schedule of the Constitution) and it should be simultaneously translated in all Indian languages. Laws of the Union Government should be made available in all Indian languages.

The CPI election manifesto of 1967[38] emphasises on the right of the people to have a linguistic state and the right of every state to use its regional language in all the domains of social life. It emphasises that it is part of the principles of democracy. Going further it states that such use of regional languages helps the India to become more integrated. As far as the use of Hindi is concerned the manifesto states that Hindi would be established as the official language only gradually and after getting the consent of non-Hindi states. As far as the regional languages are concerned the manifesto promises that they would be encouraged, developed. Attempts would be made that education till the university level can be given in the regional languages.

Election manifesto of the Socialist Party in 1962[39] says that the use of English in all government and public transactions should be stopped immediately. "That Continuation of English, the party believes is part of the Congress government's policy that reflects absence of national commitment. The manifesto further states that government correspondence should be designed in such a manner that all states would correspond with the centre in their own languages whereas the Centre will correspond with them in Hindi.

The Bharatiya Jan Sangh Election Manifesto[40] of 1956 talks about replacing English with regional languages. It announces that the Jan Sangh would develop a five-year plan to develop regional languages. It would venture to create a terminology for all Indian languages and translate writings on different disciplines in world languages in Hindi and other regional languages major literature from English.

The Bharatiya Jan Sangh Election Manifesto of 1967[41] says that the Congress Government has completely disregarded the language provisions of the Constitution and imposed English on the people. The Party aims at emancipating the people from the shackles of the English language. Its language policy includes the following things:

- Sanskrit to be declared as the country's national language and to be used on occasions of special importance.
- Immediate steps for making provincial languages the official languages of the states.
- Use of Hindi and provincial languages in those departments that come in direct contact with the people.
- Conducting of the UPSC exams in all regional languages

The Jan Sangh also promised to develop a common scientific terminology for all Indian Languages. A striking difference between the two manifestoes is that the manifesto of the CPI (M) uses the term national languages whereas the BJS manifesto uses the term provincial languages. The BJS or the BJP have not made sustained attempts for preference to locals in the public or private sector employment. For ecample, the Nirdharnama published by the BJP for 1995 Maharashtra Vidhansabha elections does not have even a single word about employment to locals or promotion of Marathi language. In the 2009 Vidhansabha elections the BJP manifesto has mentioned about development of Marathi in the domain of information technology.

The Bharatiya Jan Sangh Election Manifesto of 1971[42] talks about the constituting of a commission which would look into the creation of new states from among those areas which are affected by regional imbalances. It makes clear that independence would be incomplete without the use of people's languages. Going further, the manifesto promised that the BJS would try to make regional languages the languages of judicial business.

Coming to the recent times the election manifesto of CPI[43] for the elections of 1999 Lok Sabha mentions that all the national languages in the VIIIth schedule should be given equal status. On the contrary, the policy level statement of the Left Democratic Front for the Vidhansabha elections 2004 does not even mention the issue of language.

Various factions of the RPI have focused on the empowerment of Dalits. However, there is almost no literature available on the relationship between the empowerment of Marathi and the empowerment of Dalits. In fact, a section of Dalit civil society organisations and liberal progressive groups believe that thrust on Marathi language and its development is either urban oriented or Brahmanical in content. Therefore, it is quite obvious that they have not paid special attention to the linkage between language, culture and the Marathi Manoos. The issue at hand is whether to identify the Marathi Manoos by his linguistic identity or caste or religious identity. Many in the socialist and the communist parties believe that an overriding focus on the Marathi identity is parochial. The problem gets complicated because of the Marathi line being identified with the violent, street politics strategies adopted by Shivsena and now MNS. Many activists who swear by non-violence believe that the mainstream version of Marathi politics ignores the political economy of Maharashtra and India. They say that actually this version of politics is regressive and myopic. However, seldom have they tried to arrive at an alternate version of Marathi politics.

In the next chapter, we will deal with civil society attempts to understand the issues of Marathi language, culture and people.

Notes and References

1. For a detailed discussion of this, see Katzenstein Mary Fainsod –*Ethnicity and Equality-The Shivsena Party and preferential policies in Bombay,* Cornell University Press, Ithaca and London, 1979.
2. Quoted in Adarkar, Neera and Menon Meena- *Katha Mumbaichya Girangaochi-* Mauj Prakashan Mumbai 2007.
3. For the details of the campaign see the issues of weekly Marmik from 15th May 1966 to 16th October 1966.
4. For different aspects of the Shivsena Congress relationship see Gupta, Dipankar- *Nativism in a metropolis: Shivsena in Bombay,* (Mumbai, Manohar, 1982), pp. 175-176.
5. Joshi, Manohar, *Shivsena- Kaal, Aaj, Udya,* Prabodhan Prakashan, 2008, pp. 30-32.
6. Manohar Joshi: *Shivsena- Kaal, Aaj, Udya,* Prabodhan Prakashan, 2008, p. 176.
7. *Ibid,* p. 177.
8. Katzenstein Mary Fainsod – *Ethnicity & Equality – The Shivsena Party and Preferential Policies in Bombay,* Cornell University Press 1979, p. 146.
9. Manohar Joshi: *Shivsena- Kaal, Aaj, Udya,* Prabodhan Prakashan, 2008, pp. 188-191.
10. Interview with Sudhir Joshi, the leader of the Sthaniya Lokadhikar Samiti, May 2006.
11. Joshi, Manohar: *Shivsena- Kaal. Aaj, Udya,* Prabodhan Prakashan, 2008, p. 113.
12. For the various debates in the border dispute see Joshi, S. M. - *Mee S. M.* Continental Prakashan, Pune, 1984.
13. Joshi, Manohar: *Shivsena- Kaal. Aaj, Udya,* Prabodhan Prakashan, 2008, p. 752.
14. For the decision of the High Court of Bengaluru and the response of the Karnataka Government see http://www. prahaar. in/maharashtra/66457. html
15. Manohar Joshi: *Shivsena- Kaal, Aaj, Udya,* Prabodhan Prakashan, 2008, p. 210.
16. Manohar Joshi: *Shivsena- Kaal, Aaj, Udya,* Prabodhan Prakashan, 2008, p. 377.
17. Manohar Joshi: *Shivsena- Kaal, Aaj, Udya,* Prabodhan Prakashan, 2008, p. 644.

18. For the details of Shivsena's anti-Communism see Gupta, Dipankar - *Nativism in a metropolis: Shivsena in Bombay*, (Mumbai, Manohar, 1982), pp. 158-159.
19. Manohar Joshi: *Shivsena- Kaal, Aaj, Udya*, Prabodhan Prakashan, 2008, p. 553.
20. No. OFL-1095/737/pra. kra. 36/95-20 b reproduced in *Nyayalayin Vyavahar ani Marathi Bhasha*, Yashwantrao Chavan Pratishthan, Mumbai 1st edition, March 2007, p. 307.
21. Notification no. OFL-1098/pra. kra. 50/98/20-b b reproduced in *Nyayalayin Vyavahar ani Marathi Bhasha*, Yashwantrao Chavan Pratishthan, Mumbai 1st edition, March 2007, pp. 314-315.
22. A Circular No. p. 0104/66 dated 09. 12. 2005 was issued by the Registrar General of the High Court of Bombay expecting the lower courts to transact 50 per cent business in Marathi. This was in complete violation of the notification that was issued during the Shivsena BJP government that had ordered 100 per cent Marathikaran of the lower judiciary...However, the Shivsena legislators have not pursued this matter.
23. Shantaram Datar's Interview with the Author July 2010.
24. In an interview with the Author, eminent Shivsena leader and founder of 'Sthaniya Lokadhikar Samiti' Sudhir Joshi had mentioned had mentioned that he and his colleagues couldn't anticipate the impact of computerisation and information technology on the job market. Had they understood it, they could have prepared the Marathi youth for new areas in the job market.
25. Shivsena's political career began with controlling the Thane Municipal Corporation and later on the Bombay Municipal Corporation. It is in power in these corporations for more than a decade now. Besides that it is in power in Kalyan Dombivli Municipal Corporation, Nagpur Municipal Corporation etc.
26. The failure of Sena in BMC is more striking because Shivsena has always considered Mumbai as its stronghold. Through Sena's political control over the BMC, it could have effectively demonstrated how effective use of Marathi in administration is a double task. That required understanding of the notions of language planning which the Shivsena leadership has been generally ignorant about.
27. The details about the MNS can be found at www. manase. org . The website is in English as well as Marathi. The MNS website is the only official website of a major political party in Maharashtra that is updated on a regular basis. Other political parties are yet to see the importance of this new medium of communication with their cadre and the general public.
28. This is quite strange interpretation of the farmers' suicides in Maharashtra. That the huge influx of migration is causing strain over the resources especially in the metropolitan regions is true. But to hold it responsible for

farmers' suicides- which are caused by Government's failed agrarian policy appears farfetched.

29. For details of the attacks and the reaction to it, see Hindu, 21st October 2008 and India today of 25th October 2008.
30. The linkage between language and culture is rightly mentioned here. However, it is not really clear how MNS wishes to protect Marathi language beyond sign boards.
31. www. manase. org
32. Reported in DNA 15th August 2010 online edition. It can be accessed at http://www. dnaindia. com/mumbai/report_raj-thackeray-calls-meeting-of-marathi-producers-tomorrow_1423882.
33. In his interview with this author, Raj Thackeray spoke about making Marathi medium schools glamorous so that children and parents will be attracted to it. However, he either does not understand the importance of Marathi as a medium of instruction or does not want to appeal his cadre and common people in Maharashtra to send their children to Marathi medium schools fearing negative response from the people. (Another reason, which applies to a major section of our political elites including Raj Thackeray and Uddhav Thackeray is that they have sent their children to English medium schools and therefore find it inconvenient to appeal the people to send their children to Marathi medium schools).
34. In his interaction with this author, Raj Thackeray spoke about increasing the glamour of Marathi medium schools. It appears that he like many other Sena and MNS leaders has sent his children to the English Medium schools and therefore hesitates to take a stand on this issue.
35. Leaders of the Maharashtra Ekikaran Samiti have argued that Raj Thackeray is not aware of ground reality. There are multiple layers of organisation based on the talukas in the disputed area. Despite the differences between the N D Patil group and Kiran Thakur group, the Ekikaran Samiti is still the force to reckon with.
36. One of the reasons for the lack of proactiveness of these parties on the language issues was that they did not emerge on the Nativist agenda.
37. *The Election Manifesto of The CPI*(M), pp. 23, 24.
38. *The CPI election manifesto of 1967,* pp. 29, 31.
39. *Election manifesto of the Socialist party* in 1962, p. 12.
40. *The Bharatiya Jan Sangh Election Manifesto* page 20 published in the fifth annual conference of the BJS on 29th to 31st December 1956, Delhi.
41. *The Bharatiya Jan Sangh Election Manifesto of 1967*, pp. 12, 13.
42. *The Bharatiya Jan Sangh Election Manifesto of 1971,* pp. 17, 19 published by Bharatiya Jan Sangh, Maharashtra Pradesh.
43. *Election manifesto of the CPI,* Lok Sabha elections 1999, p. 14.

Chapter 6

Civil Society Organisations and Language Politics in Maharashtra

In the earlier chapters, we have discussed how various political parties in Maharashtra have dealt with the issues of Marathi language, culture and the Marathi speaking people. However, political parties are not the only agencies that look after these issues. Various civil society organisations have also been working on these issues. This chapter aims at evaluating the role of these organisations.

6.1 Role of CSOs

There has been a dramatic expansion in the size, scope, and capacity of civil society around the globe over the past decade, aided by the process of globalisation and the expansion of democratic governance, telecommunications, and economic integration. According to the Yearbook of International Organisations[1], the number of international NGOs was reported to have increased from 6,000 in 1990 to more than 50,000 in 2006. Civil Society Organisations (CSOs) have also become significant players in global development assistance, with the Organisation for Economic Cooperation and Development (OECD) estimating that, as of 2006, CSOs provided approximately US$15 billion in international assistance.

The civil society sector is not only emerging as a clear societal actor in many parts of the world, but it is also quite varied in its nature and composition. For this reason, definitions of civil society vary considerably based on differing conceptual paradigms, historic origins, and country context.

The World Bank[2] has adopted a definition of civil society developed by a number of leading research centers: "the term civil society to refer to the wide array of non-governmental and not-for-profit organisations that have a presence in public life, expressing the interests and values of their members or others, based on ethical, cultural, political, scientific, religious or philanthropic considerations. Civil Society Organisations (CSOs) therefore refer to a wide array of organisations: community groups, non-governmental organisations (NGOs), labour unions, indigenous groups, charitable organisations, faith-based organisations, professional associations, and foundations."

The term is often traced to Adam Ferguson[3], who saw the development of a "commercial state" as a way to change the corrupt feudal order and strengthen the liberty of the individual. While Ferguson did not draw a line between the state and the society, George Wilhelm Friedrich Hegel,[4] a German philosopher, made this distinction in his Elements of the Philosophy of Right. In this work, civil society (Hegel used the term "buergerliche Gesellschaft" though it is now referred to as Zivilgesellschaft in German to emphasise a more inclusive community) was a stage in the dialectical relationship between Hegel's perceived opposites, the macro-community of the state and the micro-community of the family. Broadly speaking, the term was split, like Hegel's followers, to the political left and right. On the left, it became the foundation for Karl Marx's bourgeois society, to the right it became a description for all non-state aspects of society, expanding out of the economic rigidity of Marxism into culture, society and politics.

6.2 CSOs in Maharashtra

Maharashtra has a strong presence of civil society organisations.

They work in various domains like education, health, gender justice, Dalit or tribal rights. Post-Emergency a number of political activists disillusioned by the moral decline of party politics decided to move towards grassroots mobilisation. This was construed to be the alternative mode of politics that is pro-people, transparent and accountable.[5] In fact, the role of such NGOs became very important and even the government agencies recognised their importance.[6] It was argued that the government needs to engage with the NGOs or voluntary organisations as they represent the various segments of the society- especially the deprived ones like Women, Adivasis, Dalits, and Children etc.[7] In a way, these organisations were considered a tool of empowerment of the masses.

The spread of NGOs in the last three decades has been overwhelming. There are local, regional, national and transnational NGOs. Many of them deal with one or more issues ranging from women's empowerment, child welfare, human rights etc. Some NGOs are engaged in constructive work whereas some others are involved in agitational activities whereas some others are engaged in both. As far as India in general and Maharashtra in particular are concerned, NGOs are guided by various ideologies ranging from Gandhism to Ambedkarism to Hindutva. The priorities of these NGOs depend on the ideologies they belong to. Although NGOs have been touted as the major tool of democratisation of politics, they have also been severely criticised for their sources of funding including foreign funding. Many of them have been criticised for changing their agenda on the basis of the changing requirements of the funding agencies.[8] It has also been argued that they carry the agenda of vested interests that are against the development in the underdeveloped countries of the world.[9] Thus, we see NGOs in the field of agriculture that are supporting opening up of the agricultural sector and those opposing it- using the same plank of development of agriculture. Post-globalisation, things have become more complex. There are NGOs that welcome it as the agency of empowerment of the masses whereas some others treat it as the agency of enslavement of people. Leaders like Sharad Joshi of the

Shetkari Sanghatana have criticised NGOs for projecting themselves as the liberators of people and making them dependent. He argues that after the collapse of the Soviet Union the spread of NGOs has increased. Although they talk of environment, sustainable development and equitable distribution of resources, they are actually anti-freedom that has been brought on by the end of socialism.[10] Whether the NGOs are a genuine representation of the society or whether they are hegemonic in nature is again a matter of serious debate.

Although there are innumerable organisations in Maharashtra working in the domain of agriculture, education, Dalit rights, women's empowerment etc., there are not many in the domain of language and culture.

Traditionally, it is perceived that there is no major difference between development of language and development of literature. Therefore, literary organisations like Sahitya Parishads are supposed to look into the development of Marathi language. A cursory look at the activities of the various Parishads suggests that their core competence lies in issues related to literary criticism, poetry recitation and related activities. Although issues of language are discussed, it is rather at a superior level. Akhil Bhartiya Sahitya Mahamandal is the apex body of literary organisations in and outside Maharashtra. One of the major events organised by the Mahamandal is the Akhil Bhartiya Marathi Sahitya Sammelan (All India Marathi Literary Conference). This is a popular event in the literary world and members of the literati compete with each other to control these events and also to become the President of the Sammelan.

6.3 Sahitya Parishads and Language Development

Of late, these Sammelans have become an expensive affair and the expenditure is anywhere between 75 lakhs to one crore. The Government of Maharashtra through the Sahitya Sanskruti Mandal gives Rs 25 lakh rupees to the Sammelan every year. Generally, the chief organisers of the Sammelan are local politicians from different parties. They are roped in with the clear intent of collecting sufficient money for the Sammelan. In return, they occupy sizeable space in the opening and concluding ceremony. Although there are a number of seminars in a sammelan, majority of them are devoted to literary issues. The speech of the president of the Sammelan is an opportunity to discuss language related issues. But with rare exceptions, the presidents have not spoken on pressing language issues.[11] At the end of every Sammelan, a number of resolutions are passed. Language issues do find a place here. These resolutions address the issues of medium of instruction, use of Marathi in administration, judiciaries etc. But the resolutions are not taken seriously either by those who make them or by those who are supposed to act on them. Thus, Sammelans cannot contribute substantively to language issues.

Besides the Akhil Bhartiya Marathi Sahitya Sammelan, there are various regional, sub-regional caste-based Sammelans. Important among them is the Vidrohi Sahitya Sammelan. It is generally organised as the challenge to the Akhil Bhartiya Marathi Sahitya Sammelan. It claims that Akhil Bhartiya Marathi Sahitya Sammelan represents only the Brahmanical interests and is therefore not representative. Even the Vidrohi Sahitya Sammelan majorly devotes its time to issues of literary criticism. Thus, the whole exercise of conducting various Sahitya Sammelans does not do much good to Marathi language. For last few years, Akhil Bhartiya Sahitya Mahamandal organises Vishva Marathi Sahitya Sammelans outside India. The idea is to bring together nonresident Maharashtrians in different parts of the world and spread Marathi literature. The president of this Sahitya Sammelan is not elected, but chosen unanimously by the various wings of the Mahamandal. Again, the focus areas of discussion are literature and criticism. Only recently, Mahesh Elkunchwar, eminent playwright and president of the Vishva Marathi Sahitya Sammelan held at Singapore spoke about the problems of Marathi at length. Barring such speeches, the discussions in these Sammelans are purely literary in nature. Overall, the role of literary organisations and the programmes organised by them does not take serious note of language issues, nor have they been able to come out with an action plan for such issues.[12]

One of the major problems created by the way our literary agencies are handled is that confusion of the political leaders as well as literary figures about issues of literary development and issues of language development has further deepened. A section of the literary elites strongly believes that spread of literature will automatically lead to development of language. Linguists however argue to the contrary. They believe that development of literature is a small part of language development. A language can really develop when it flourishes in the non-literary domains like education, administration, judiciary, technology etc. Such initiatives require specialised efforts, which may not be the strength of litterateurs. Unfortunately, in Maharashtra functions of literary and language development are not just confused, they are routinely handed over to authors who either do not understand the work or end up doing it through the prism of literature thus spoiling language development institutions.

6.4 CSOs Dedicated to Language Issues[13]

Another category of Civil Society Organisations are those specifically dedicated to some issues of Marathi language. Although a number of individuals have dedicated themselves to the cause of preservation of Marathi language, organisational efforts are few.

Marathi Bhasha Sanrakshan and Vikas Sanstha was established in the Year 2000 although Datar and his colleagues were working on language issues even prior to that by Shantaram Datar, a lawyer. The aim of the organisation was to ensure that entire business in local courts in Maharashtra is conducted in Marathi. Datar and his lawyer colleagues organised gatherings, dharnas, and morchas in order to draw the attention of the government and the legal fraternity. Datar worked closely with the Department of Law and Judiciary, Government of Maharashtra in order to draft the notification that made Marathi the language of the local courts. Unfortunately, the

High Court of Mumbai did not act upon the notification issued in July 1998 by the Government of Maharashtra until 2005. In December 2005, the High Court issued a circular that said that minimum 50 per cent of the judgments of the district and taluka courts should be in Marathi. This was in clear contradiction with the July 1998 notification that makes it mandatory for the local courts to transact their entire business in Marathi.

Datar has participated in various gatherings of lawyers and expressed disappointment over this avoidable delay. He also campaigns for making Marathi the authorised language of the High Court of Mumbai under Article 348(2). It has already been noted in the previous chapter (nos 2 & 4) that States of the North have declared Hindi as the authorised language of their respective High Courts since 1970. Legislative Assemblies of States like Tamil Nadu, West Bengal have unanimously passed a resolution making their official languages the authorised languages of their respective High Courts. However, the Government of Maharashtra has not taken any proactive steps in this direction. Datar has also contributed towards translation of important case laws. He was an active member of the now defunct Vidhi Anuvad ani Paribhasha Sallagar Samiti (Advisory Committee for legal translation and terminology designing) which was assigned the task of preparing authorised texts of central laws. The committee functioned under the General administration Department. However, due to the non-serious attitude of the government, the committee could not do much work. Presently Datar is involved into translation and publication for the Maharashtra Law Journal. He believes that Marathi has the potential to become Dnyan Bhasha or the language of knowledge provided proper efforts are made in that direction.[14] Occasionally, he writes for newspapers and participates in conferences on Marathi in judiciary. The work of his organisation is confined to Thane district. Participation of lawyers in the organisation is notional in nature. Datar has interacted with the political leaders and has participated in various legislative advocacy activities. However, his efforts to strengthen the organisation have not really succeeded.

Anil Gore runs 'Samartha Marathi' organisation from Pune. He is actively involved in the campaign for use of Marathi on signboards, use of Marathi in Banks, making Marathi available as the medium of instruction for the students of science faculty at the H.S.C. level etc.[15] This group too has a limited organisational wherewithal. Gore participates in various Sammelans and campaigns through posters designed for the purpose or even wearing T- Shirts with slogans related to promotion of Marathi. He has interacted with members of the political fraternity and pushed for certain issues through the State Legislature. He has started the Prati Dnyaneshwar project through which he attempts to bring important science texts into Marathi.

Marathi Ekjoot is a group established by Saleel Kulkarni, Vijay Padhye and others from Pune.[16] It was established as a discussion forum of various organisations working for Marathi. Saleel Kulkarni, one of the founders had written articles in Loksatta, a leading Marathi Daily as a precursor to the first meeting of this group. These meetings are not well attended. There is no organisation in place on the ground. Much of the work of this group is done through the exchange of e-mails. The actual impact of this group is very limited, at best.

Kantaram Sonawane[17] established Marathi Janaadhikar Parishad in January 2003 with the demand that 80 per cent in all sectors be reserved for Maharashtrians. The demand per se is not new. Shivsena had raised this demand in the 1960s and achieved some results. The Janaadhikar Parishad was raising this demand post-globalisation. Sonawane organised few meetings of like-minded people. However, without any organisational back up, he made an attempt to use the organisation as a political instrument which failed. The movement fizzled out within few months.

Prabhakar Purandare and late Rajendra Phadke ran a splinter group called Marathi Mahasangh. The objective was to empower Marathi speaking people with grassroots mobilisation. It organised door to door campaigns in BDD Chawls of Worli in 2002, Mumbai.

However, the campaign did not yield much result. Through press conferences the group also raised the issue of migrants in Mumbai and the policy of the Railway ministry then controlled by the North Indian leadership to run trains from the northern states to Mumbai for the benefit of the migrant workers. Their argument was that it is a matter of political design on the part of the various leaders of UP and Bihar who were Railway Ministers, to increase the number of trains from these states to Mumbai and other parts of Maharashtra so as to facilitate the huge influx of migrants from the backward areas of these states to the metropolitan areas in Maharashtra. However, due to the death of Rajendra Phadke in 2008 and the declining health of Prabhakar Purandare, the group is in disarray.

Sanjay Bhide and others started an organisation called Amhi Marathi through which they organised programmes like welcoming the Marathi New Year through cultural programmes. The group organises monthly meetings. However, the organisation has not undertaken any major issue so far.

Dr Datta Pawar is a retired principal who started Marathi Anyay Nirmulan Parishad (Conference against injustice on Marathi) in the late 1970s when Marathi as a subject was removed from undergraduate courses of science and commerce faculties. When he initiated the struggle with the help of teachers and literary figures in Marathi, the movement did not last long due to the apathy of the elites.[18] Presently he runs Marathi Sanshodhan Mandal which publishes Marathi Sanshodhan Patrika – a magazine devoted to literary and linguistic issues. Satvasheela Samant is a retired government employee from the Directorate of Languages. She devotes her time on issues like Varnamala, Pramanlekhan etc.

Among the literary bodies, a pleasant exception is that of Marathi Abhyas Parishad founded by among others Dr Ashok Kelkar, eminent linguist. It publishes a reputed academic quarterly journal Bhasha ani Jeevan (Language and life) which discusses various issues of contemporary relevance. The editorial team has written extensively on the language policies (or the lack of it) of the Government of Maharashtra and has occasionally participated in campaigns as well. However, the circulation of the journal is very limited. Besides, there are not many young persons who can carry forward this work.

B.Y. Gadgil,[19] a scholar has written a book on the idea of autonomous Maharashtra. He talks about the marginalisation of Maharashtrians in Maharashtra and tries to search the cause of it in the political economy of the State. He tries to contest the idea of Indian nationalism and argues for the demand of autonomous Maharashtra. However, he clarifies that this is not a demand for secession but restructuring of Indian federation. He initiated Swayatta Maharashtra Samiti (Committee for the autonomy of Maharashtra) after the publication of his book. However, the idea has very few takers.

Another short lived venture was undertaken by a committee of teachers and journalists when the Government of Maharashtra decided to introduce information technology as an option to Marathi at the 11th and 12th Standards in June 2001. They did not oppose the introduction of Information Technology. The criticism was about making it an option to Marathi. Meetings were conducted, Dharnas were organised, and celebrities were roped in. Through street plays and folklore, the issue was brought on the radar of the media. However, the government argued that the teachers of the Marathi subject are criticising a good, progressive and pro Bahujan decision of the government because they were afraid of losing their jobs. The then minister for school education, Ramkrishna More turned the whole debate into upper caste conspiracy to deprive the Bahujan Samaj of information technology.[20]

Even the Marathi media was divided on this issue. The leader of the movement, the then editor of Daily Mahanagar Nikhil Wagle from Mumbai and Professor G.N. Joglekar of the Akhil Bhartiya Marathi Sahitya Sammelan had heated arguments with Ramkrishna More, Kapil Patil the editor of Daily Aaj Dinank and Aroon Tikekar, the editor of Loksatta.[21] In the Akhil Bhartiya Marathi Sahitya

Sammelan held at Pune, the agitators organised Dharnas and demanded that they be allowed to participate in the seminar on the status of Marathi language in Maharashtra. This permission was granted reluctantly, Mr Wagle insisted that he be allowed to speak after the minister. That went against the protocol and hence was not accepted. When the Minister started speaking, Mr Wagle and few others shouted slogans and were dragged by the police. The agitators lost an opportunity to present their case before the common people of Maharashtra. Soon, the agitation lost its momentum. The government rejected the demand of the agitators.[22]

6.5 Marathi Abhyas Kendra (MAK)

Teachers, lawyers and journalists established Marathi Abhyas Kendra (MAK) in 2007 of which this researcher is also a part.[23] Members of this organisation have been working on issues of Marathi language and culture since 2002.They came together so that it would be possible to work simultaneously on multiple issues. These members also wanted to concentrate on research on language policy, while continuing the agitation on such issues. MAK functions through various action groups. They are:

- ***Database Group*** – Generating Database of individuals and institutions working or willing to work for the promotion of Marathi language and culture. Developing a steady network of activists and researchers through this network.
- ***Research group*** – Undertaking independent or collaborative research projects that would help in building a knowledge base for the preservation of Marathi language and culture.
- ***Marathi medium schools and colleges empowerment group*** - Developing Marathi as a medium of instruction and strengthening Marathi schools.
- ***A Group for Economic networking of Marathi speaking people*** - Use of Marathi in various employment areas, making industrial and business-related training modules in Marathi. Bringing together various stakeholders of the economy for this.

- ***Marathi Institutions group*** - Bringing together Marathi departments and Marathi Language and Literary Associations from various colleges and Universities across Maharashtra on a common platform for collaborative action. Networking with various language and literature related agencies across Maharashtra.
- ***Right to Information Group*** - Using the RTI for understanding the status of use of Marathi in different domains of social life and pressurising the government through the information made available by such correspondence.
- ***Information Technology and Marathi Group*** - Empowering Marathi with the help of Information and Communication Technology. Using the Internet for the promotion of Marathi. Training the common people for using Marathi on the Computer and the Internet.
- ***Use of Marathi in the Judiciary*** - Ensuring the use of Marathi in the lower Judiciary and giving her the status of authorised language of the High Court of the State. Networking with the concerned agencies for the implementation of pending issues in this regard.

Following are some of the Campaigns of MAK:

- Campaign for strengthening of the Directorate of Language and other language-related agencies that culminated in the creation of the Marathi Bhasha Vibhag (Marathi Language Department) in the Golden Jubilee year of the creation of the state of Maharashtra.
- Campaigning for the use of Unicode[24] (a system that provides level playing field to Non English Languages on Computers and in the Cyberspace). Following up the issue with the Government of Maharashtra, Local self-government institutions, software companies like Microsoft, government agencies like CDAC (Centre for Development of Advanced Technology) and NIC (National Informatics

Centre). Organising training workshops for the promotion of Unicode.

- Developing an action plan for the empowerment of Marathi medium schools.
- Sending proposals and arranging seminars with Vice Chancellors of different Universities in Maharashtra for modifying the syllabi of the Marathi subject and introduce courses in applied Marathi and linguistics.
- Coordinating with the local courts and the High Court in the state for entire Marathikaran of the lower Judiciary and making Marathi the authorised language of the High Court of Bombay according to Article 348(2) of the Constitution.
- Using RTI to get information about the use of Marathi in Central Government establishments in Maharashtra, Banks and Mobile Companies. Using such information to pressurise the concerned agencies and institutions to increase the use of Marathi in respective domains.
- Making Marathi Language and Literary Associations mandatory in the Mumbai University and affiliated colleges.
- Making various professional courses available in Marathi. The first among them was the Three Year Bachelor of Mass Media course of the Mumbai University.

MAK could be described as the first genuinely multi-functional organisation in that it tries to understand the dynamics of Marathi language and culture in the light of the contemporary reality in Maharashtra. However, it is not a mass movement yet, although its ideology has the potential of developing into one.

6.6 Analysing the Role of Civil Society Organisations

All these organisations have used various instruments to pursue their agenda. Some of them are as follows:

1. Writing letters, petitions to the government, semi-government authorities.

2. Collaborating with like-minded organisations to pursue a matter and sensitise people over language issues.
3. Seeking information under the Right to Information about the use or non-use of Marathi in various domains and using this information as a tool for campaigning.
4. Lobbying with political parties and their students units, trade unions wings and providing them inputs on the basis of which parties can make language policies.
5. Advocacy in the legislature, raise questions through individual MLAs who may show interest on certain issues either due to taking up of these issues by the media or to take the ruling parties to task.
6. Proactive use of the media: In this case, media is not just a tool for publicity campaign but it participates in the campaign as one of the stakeholders. The political elites whether in the ruling party or in the opposition have to take cognizance of such campaigns because of the fear of adverse publicity from the media. When media persons gel well into the campaign, they volunteer on their own for advocacy efforts. Marathi Abhyas Kendra's (MAK) campaign about the declining position of the directorate of language and other language agencies of Government of Maharashtra would be a good case study in this regard. While campaigning about the defunct nature of language agencies in Maharashtra, the MAK team networked extensively with media persons in the Marathi media. The delegations that met the director of language, Deputy Chief Minister and Chief Minister of Maharashtra, included senior editors and journalists. This put tremendous on the government. In the process, the media persons started owning this cause and published stories on their own. It is due to this pressure that the government of Maharashtra was forced to establish a separate department for Marathi. A not so brighter side of this engagement is the consequent

disinterestedness of the media. Therefore, advocacy efforts have to be continued not only through the media but they are a useful instrument for keeping the media on its toes.

There are various advantages and disadvantages of these instruments. Advantages are as follows:

(a) If one campaign using a certain instrument gets success, the same instrument may be used by others thus increasing the pace of activism.

(b) Some of these groups have been recognised as pressure groups on language issues. Opinions of such organisations are taken into consideration during media debates or while drafting manifestos of political parties.

(c) Success with one agency may mean that other similar agencies follow suit. For example, one mobile operator makes the Marathi option available in the IVR system, other mobile operators may follow suit. However, one should be warned against idealism because the corporate sector is generally apathetic to local languages.

(d) Such campaigns require minimum human and material resources. With the spread of information and communication technology, campaigning and canvassing has become less expensive. Thus, a sustained campaign can achieve visible results with minimum resources and it can open the field for many such smaller, local and low cost initiatives.

However, such initiatives also have limitations;

(a) Organisations with limited resources can take up only one issue at a time. Thus, the number of issues addressed at a time would be very less.

(b) Deciding procedures for activism remains voluntary. Under these circumstances, professional strategising may be lacking in such organisations.

(c) Various initiatives may get symbolic or occasionally even real success but penetrating the political system and bringing about macro policy changes sometimes becomes difficult.

(d) Civil society organisations have an option to join a political party and carry their agenda forward. However, that may compromise their autonomy. More importantly, the perspective of mainstream political parties working for Marathi language and the approach of many civil society organisations is not similar. More so, civil society organisations do not have a common platform to strengthen themselves and avoid duplication of work. Thus, civil society organisations are caught between the devil and the deep sea. Efforts have been made by Marathi Abhyas Kendra and Marathi Ekjoot to bring together civil society activists working for Marathi language. However, these efforts have not borne fruit.

Notes and References

1. The Yearbook can be accessed at http://www. uia. be/yearbook
2. The details can be accessed at http://web. worldbank. org/WBSITE/ EXTERNAL/TOPICS/CSO/0, content MDK:20101499~menu PK:244752~pagePK:220503~piPK:220476~ theSitePK:228717, 00. html
3. Adam Ferguson's '*An Essay on History of Civil Society*' (1767) can be accessed at http://www. constitution. org/af/civil. htm
4. Full text of Hegel's Elements of the Philosophy of Right can be accessed at http://www. marxists. org/reference/archive/hegel/works/pr/printrod. htm
5. For a detailed discussion of the NGOS see Dharmadhikari Avinash-Aswastha Dashakachi Diary, Unmesh Prakashan, 1989.
6. From the Seventh Five Year Plan onwards, the Government of India formally tried to collaborate with the NGO sector through bodies like CAPART (Council for Advancement of People's Action and Rural technology). For details see http://capart. nic. in/
7. A detailed list of NGOs in Maharashtra could be found at http://www. maharashtra. ngosindia. com/
8. For example see a speech by Sharad Joshi leader of Shetkari Sanghatana in a national seminar on 'Natural resources and Human Rights Struggles' organised by K. J. Somaiya College of Arts and Commerce, Mumbai, Vidyaviha, 8-9 Dec. 2006.

9. Argument made by Dabholkar, Dattaprasad in Mate Narmade (Rajhans Prakashan, Pune, 2004)in the context of the Narmada dam conflict.
10. Joshi Sharad, *ibid.*
11. Every year the Akhil Bhartiya Marathi Sahitya Mahamandal and the organisation hosting the Sammelan jointly publish the full text of the speech of the President of the Sahitya Sammelan. Excerpts from the speech are also published in all leading Marathi dailies.
12. For a detailed reporting of the Singapore Sahitya Sammelan see the article by Usha Tambe, President Akhil Bhartiya Sahitya Mahamandal at http:// maharashtratimes. indiatimes. com/articleshow/9742521. cms
13. The analysis in this section is primarily based on extensive interactions this researcher has had with persons involved in these CSOs. As one of the founder member of Marathi Abhyas Kendra (MAK), this researcher has had various opportunities to interact with persons in CSOs with similar objectives.
14. Personal interview with the author, Dec. 2010.
15. The details about this campaign and some reactions to it can be accessed at http://mr. upakram. org/node/2633
16. The background of the formation of this organisation can be found in the two articles written by Saleel Kulkarni in Loksatta dated 15th and 20th November 2009. They can be accessed at http://amrutmanthan. wordpress. com/2009/11/15/%E0%A4%B9%E0%A4%BF%E0%A4%82%E0%A4%A6%E0%A5%80-%E0%A4%B9%E0%A5%80-%E0%A4%B0%E0%A4%BE%E0%A4%B7%E0%A5%8D%E0%A4%9F%E0%A5%8D%E0%A4%B0%E0%A4%AD%E0%A4%BE%E0%A4%B7% E0%A4%BE-%E0%A4%8F%E0%A4%95-%E0%A4%9A/

    And http://amrutmanthan. wordpress. com/2009/12/21/%E0%A4%8F% E0% A4%95%E0%A4%9A-%E0%A4%85%E0%A4%AE%E0%A5%8B%E0% A4%98 %E0%A4%89%E0%A4%AA%E0%A4%BE%E0%A4%AF-%E0%A4%AE%E0%A4%B0%E0%A4%BE%E0%A4%A0%E0%A5%80-%E0%A4%8F%E0%A4%95%E0%A4%9C%E0%A5%82%E0%A4%9F/
17. The details of the establishment of the Parishad and its demands can be found at http://maharashtratimes. indiatimes. com/articleshowarchive. cms?msid=38592157
18. For details of the debate see Pawar, Datta-*Marathi Bhasha:Apeksha ani Upeksha,* Sahityasanwad Prakashan, Mumbai, December, 1996.
19. Gadgil, B. Y., *Haak Swayatta Maharashtrachi,* 2nd edition, Granthali, 1999.
20. The entire argument of the Government of Maharashtra on this issue is presented in a booklet titled "*Abhyaskramat Mahiti Tantradnyan-Shasanachi Bhumika*- Shaleya Shikshan Vibhag, Maharashtra Shasan,

Mumbai January 2002. This booklet was circulated to the general public in the Akhil Bhartiya Marathi Sahitya Sammelan held at Pune in January 2002. A booklet countering this argument was also published. See Bagle, Prabhakar (Ed.), *Haddaparichya Waatewaril Marathi*- Anushtubh Pratishthan, Mumbai January, 2002.

21. For details of the debate see Editorials and edit page articles in Loksatta and Mahanagar between 0ctober 2001 and January 2002.
22. Long term impact of the failure of this agitation can be seen in the following news item. http://www. esakal. com/esakal/20120228/5631117402250620229. htm
23. The organisation's headquarters is located in Thane. Its registration No. is MAH/694/Thane & Registration no. with the Charity Commissioner is F/18501/ Thane. Website: www. marathivikas. org
24. The details about Unicode and its role in empowerment of languages in Information and Communication Technology can be accessed at http://unicode. org/

Chapter 7

New Politics of Marathi in the Age of Globalisation

7.1 Marathikaaran- An Introduction

Language is essentially a political issue and therefore it has to be suitably handled through a language-based political movement. Such a movement has to develop a linkage between Marathi language, culture and economic interests of the Marathi speaking people. Henceforth, this ideology would be described as '*Marathi-kaaran*' – Politics and economics of Marathi language, culture and *Marathi Manoos*. The previous chapters have analysed the limitations of the government, political parties as well as civil society organisations in seeking such an ambitious language agenda. Such a movement needs to have the following tenets:

- Generating consciousness about the importance of Marathi language and culture among the Marathi speaking people.
- Emphasising Marathi language as the core component of Maharashtrian and such an identity to be the basis for political mobilisation of the Marathi speaking people.
- Linking the usage of Marathi language in different domains of social life for the Empowerment of the Marathi speaking people.
- Developing Marathi as the language of knowledge and employment through sustained, institutionalised efforts.

- Keeping intact the integrity of Maharashtra by facilitating organic unity amongst various sub-regions of Maharashtra. This can be done by astutely handling the issue of regional imbalance.
- Developing institutional mechanisms for the promotion of Marathi language and culture in the governmental, non-governmental and civil society arena.
- Clearly linking the issues of Marathi language and culture to various social struggles.

7.2 Aims of Marathikaaran

The movement of Marathikaaran will have to aim at:

- Implementation of Constitutional provisions regarding the empowerment of Indian languages (in this case the empowerment of Marathi).
- Implementation of various provisions regarding the development of Marathi that have been enacted since the creation of Unified Maharashtra.
- Developing suitable institutional mechanisms for the promotion of Marathi language and culture.
- Enhancing the collaboration between the government and non-government institutions for developing a comprehensive plan for the development of Marathi language and culture.
- Evolving a constructive, substantive framework for the development of Marathi language and culture which can facilitate the emergence of mass movement that is not merely reactive and symbolic in nature.
- Ensuring that this movement categorically avoids recourse to violence.
- Preserve the linguistic rights of minorities while ensuring the rights of majority Maharashtrians.

Marathikaaran defined this way needs a definite plan of action which is discussed in the next chapter. Here I provide a rationale for Marathikaaran.

While it is true that mere state initiative or intervention can't ensure the development of a language, it must be noted that nowhere in the contemporary world have languages survived or flourished without state help-English being the greatest example of such initiative.[1] Throughout the world countries have been engaged in all out efforts of language planning ensuring functional allocation of languages in different domains of language. From China, Indonesia in Asia to France, Germany in Europe to the United States almost every country is into the business of language planning.[2] Whether they accept unilingual, bilingual or trilingual policies depend upon their peculiar conditions. The fact that no state has shunned the responsibility of language planning shows that it is an integral part of modern governance. Unfortunately, in India the issue has not been given as much importance as it should. In fact, there appears to be a sense of awkwardness both among academicians and policy-makers about this. The reasons for this may lie in the bloodshed witnessed after partition based on religious nationalism and the consequent fear that linguistic reorganisation of states would lead to similar clashes. After the linguistic reorganisation of states (the process that continued till the 1970s), various states did undertake initiatives for the development of their respective official languages. Various acts were passed by state governments to ensure increased use of official languages in the states.[3] However, there was a huge gap between the pace of legislation and the requirements of language planning. The use of Marathi in state administration, judiciary, education and technology still remained a distant goal. The reasons as discussed in the chapter on Congress in Maharashtra lie in flawed understanding of language development.

It is useful in this context to understand the idea of language planning and see how it can be applied to Maharashtra.

7.3 Language Planning

Language planning is a deliberate effort to influence the function, structure, or acquisition of languages or language variety within a speech community. It is often associated with government planning, but is also used by a variety of non-governmental organisations, such as grass-roots organisations and even individuals. The goals of language planning differ depending on the nation or organisation, but generally include making planning decisions and possibly changes for the benefit of communication. Planning or improving effective communication can also lead to other social changes such as language shift or assimilation, thereby providing another motivation to plan the structure, function and acquisition of languages.[4]

Following issues motivate decision-making in language planning:

- ***Linguistic assimilation*** - the belief that every member of a society, irrespective of his native language, should learn and use the dominant language of the society in which he/she lives. A quintessential example is the English-only movement in the United States.
- ***Linguistic pluralism***[5] - the recognition and support of multiple languages within one society. Apart from India, the examples include the coexistence of French, German, Italian, and Romansh in Switzerland and the shared status of English, Malay, Tamil, and Chinese in Singapore. Vernacularisation- the restoration and development of an indigenous language along with its adoption by the state as an official language. Examples include Hebrew in the state of Israel and Quechua in Peru.
- ***Internationalisation***- the adoption of a non-indigenous language of wider communication as an official language or in a particular domain, such as the use of English in Singapore, India, the Philippines etc.

Language planning has been divided into three types:[6]

- ***Status planning***

  Status planning is the allocation or reallocation of a language or variety to functional domains within a society, thus affecting the status, or standing, of a language.

- ***Corpus planning***

  Corpus planning refers to the prescriptive intervention in the forms of a language, whereby planning decisions are made to engineer changes in the structure of the language. Corpus planning activities often arise as the result of beliefs about the adequacy of the form of a language to serve desired functions. Unlike status planning, which is primarily undertaken by administrators and politicians, corpus planning generally involves planners with greater linguistic expertise. There are three traditionally recognised types of corpus planning: graphisation, standardisation, and modernisation.

- ***Acquisition planning***

  Acquisition planning is a type of language planning in which a national, state or local government system aims to influence aspects of language, such as language status, distribution and literacy through education. Acquisition planning can also be used by non-governmental organisations, but it is more commonly associated with government planning. Frequently, acquisition planning is integrated into a larger language planning process in which the positions of languages are evaluated, corpuses are revised and the changes are finally introduced to society on a national, state or local level through education systems, ranging from primary schools to universities.

7.4 Language Policy

Many countries or regions within a country have a language policy designed to favour or discourage the use of a particular language or set of languages. Although nations historically have used language policies most often to promote one official language at the expense of others, many countries now have policies designed to protect and promote regional and ethnic languages whose viability is threatened.[7] Language policy is what a government does either officially through legislation, court decisions or policy to determine how languages are used, cultivate language skills needed to meet national priorities or to establish the rights of individuals or groups to use and maintain languages.[8]

7.5 Linguistic Rights

Language rights or linguistic human rights are the human and civil rights concerning the individual and collective right to choose the language or languages for communication in a private or public atmosphere. Linguistic rights include, among others, the right to one's own language in legal, administrative and judicial acts, language education, and media in a language understood and freely chosen by those concerned. Linguistic rights in international law are usually dealt in the broader framework of cultural and educational rights. Important documents for linguistic rights include the Universal Declaration of Linguistic Rights, the European Charter for Regional or Minority Languages and the Framework Convention for the Protection of National Minorities. Most of the initial literature on linguistic rights came from countries where linguistic and/or national divisions grounded in linguistic diversity have resulted in linguistic rights playing a vital role in maintaining stability. However, it was not until the 1900s that linguistic rights gained official status in politics and international accords.

Linguistic rights were first included as an international human right in the Universal Declaration of Human Rights in 1948.

Some make a distinction between Language Rights and Linguistic Human Rights because the former concept covers a much wider scope.[9] Thus, not all language rights are LHR, although all LHR are language rights. One way of distinguishing language rights from LHR is between what is necessary, and what is enrichment-oriented. Necessary rights, as in human rights, are those needed for basic needs and for living a dignified life, e.g. language-related identity, access to mother tongue(s), right of access to an official language, no enforced language shift, access to formal primary education based on language, and the right for minority groups to perpetuate as a distinct group, with own languages. Enrichment rights are above basic needs, e.g. right to learn foreign languages.

As mentioned earlier, language policies are generally governed by language regulators. They are supposed to supervise the usage of languages in a society and develop policies and programmes for the empowerment of a language.[10]

Bòrd na Gàidhlig, Dutch Language Union, Foras na Gaeilge, Office Québécois de la langue française, Welsh Language Board, Pan South African Language Board are some of the language regulators that look after the development and promotion in their respective countries.

For example, Bòrd na Gàidhlig was established as a public body by the Gaelic Language (Scotland) Act 2005 which was commenced on 13th February 2006. The legislation is designed to promote the use of Scottish Gaelic, secure the status of the language and ensure its long-term future. The Act sets out three main aims for Bòrd na Gàidhlig:

1. To increase the number of persons who are able to use and understand the Gaelic language;
2. To encourage the use and understanding of the Gaelic language; and
3. To facilitate access, in Scotland and elsewhere, to the Gaelic language and Gaelic culture. As a statutory Non-departmental Public Body, the Bòrd is directly funded by the Scottish Ministers and is accountable to them. The Bòrd works closely with the Scottish Government, public authorities and key partners, including the Gaelic organisations and community groups, to promote and develop the use and understanding of Gaelic and to ensure that public funds are wisely and effectively spent. Bòrd na Gàidhlig, in partnership with Gaelic speakers and the people of Scotland, wants Gaelic to be spoken far and wide.[11]

The Dutch Language Union and The Netharlandse Taalunie[12] work for the promotion of Dutch language in various countries. It looks into

- sharing the task of developing expensive language aids, such as reference works.
- pooling expertise and sharing ideas on the teaching of Dutch.
- providing in-service training for teachers of Dutch and literary translators.
- developing a language policy within the European context.

In India, the idea of language regulator is not taken very seriously. Although the Department of Official Language in the Ministry of Home Affairs looks after the usage of Hindi in various domains of social life, there is no agency to look after the development of all the languages included in the eighth schedule of the constitution. The Government of Maharashtra in a proactive step decided to establish the Rajya Marathi Vikas Sanstha (State Institute for the Development of Marathi) as the authorised language agency in 1993. However, it was not adequately empowered.

It is on this backdrop that we will try to understand how Maharashtra can adopt policies and programmes that will not only help overcome the present stalemate over language politics, but also create institutional mechanisms for the promotion of Marathi language and culture. A *Roadmap* is suggested here.

7.6 Establishment of the Department of Language

The establishment of a separate Department for the development of Marathi Language within the Government of Maharashtra has begun the process of planning. However, the department needs to be more broad-based in its structure and functions. To develop Marathi language as a social resource (like land, water and energy) and to establish a permanent, transparent and accountable agency for the development of Marathi would be the objective of the department if it is to be an effective language regulator. The broad area of operation for the department would include the following:

I. Undertaking multi-pronged efforts for the development of Marathi as the language of daily usage, administration and advanced fields of knowledge.

II. Developing resources for enhancing the use of Marathi in the fields of agriculture, medicine, industry, trade, commerce, science, technology, media etc. Developing language-based technologies for various domains of social life.

III. Undertaking time bound linguistic surveys and preparing status reports about Marathi.

IV. Undertaking programmes to enhance the use of Marathi in government and semi-government undertakings to make the use of Marathi people oriented.

V. Developing terminologies for generation of new knowledge in Marathi.

VI. To make Marathi language inclusive and accommodative by building bridges between the language of the elites and the various dialects of the masses.

VII. Developing suitable computer and web based technologies for the enhanced use of Marathi in Information and Communication Technology.

VIII. Developing resources for the Non-Maharashtrians staying in Maharashtra so that they get an opportunity to learn Marathi language and understand about Marathi culture.

The list of broad areas mentioned above is not exhaustive. It will change as per the need of the situation. The primary task of the department would be to publish white papers on the status of Marathi in the fields of education (from primary to the university level), Judiciary, administration, information and communication technology, trade and commerce, science and technology, economy etc. Rajya Marathi Vikas Sanstha could be declared as the authorised agency for the development of the Marathi language. It is through this nodal agency that the department should coordinate its functions of language planning. The department should have a cabinet rank minister assisted by a minister of state. The Director of Rajya Marathi Vikas Sanstha should be given the status of minister of state and all other agencies of language development should function under it.

The Department of Official Language of the Government of India has a parliamentary committee that looks after the usage of Hindi at various levels of administration. It is authorised to make recommendations and suggest punitive action against errant officials. Similarly, a committee of the Maharashtra State Legislature would be appointed to look into the use of Marathi in state as well as central government establishments. The committee would be authorised to visit concerned departments and suggest action against errant officials. The Department of Marathi Language would be given the responsibility of time bound implementation of the recommendations of the committee.

7.7 Present Structure of the Department

- Rajya Marathi Vikas Sanstha (State Institute for the development of Marathi).
- Maharashtra Rajya Sahitya Sanskruti Mandal (Maharashtra state board for literature and culture).
- Maharashtra Rajya Vishvakosh Nirmiti Mandal (Maharashtra state board for Encyclopedia in Marathi).
- Bhasha Sanchalanalay (Directorate of Language).

7.8 Proposed Structure of the Department

The proposed structure would include two more agencies. They would be Vidyapeeth Granthnirmiti Mandal- a body that was devised for developing university level texts in Marathi. (It is presently defunct) and Granthalay Sanchalanalay (Directorate of Libraries, which is presently under the Department of Higher and Technical Education) which is presently under the Department of Higher and

Technical Education. Besides these agencies, an array of new target driven agencies may be created so that the department becomes competent and comprehensive. There may be seven new sub-units within the Department of Marathi and they would look after specified tasks. The sub-units and their work profile are given below.

- ***Section working on Marathi as medium of instruction and the expansion of Marathi education***
    - Providing quality education in all disciplines in Marathi
    - Encouraging and empowering Marathi medium schools and colleges.
    - Bridging the gap between education in English and Marathi medium in terms of utility and quality and making it employment driven.
    - Improving the scope and quality of teaching of Marathi in English medium schools.
    - Preparing Status about Marathi medium schools.
    - Improving the quality of teaching of English and information technology in Marathi medium schools. Making adequate budgetary provisions for the same.
    - Revising the policy on granting permissions to English Medium schools in an indiscriminate manner.
    - Improving the quality of teaching in D.Ed, B.Ed and M.Ed colleges.
    - Encouraging public-private partnership to develop parallel and supplementary books.
    - Initiating the establishment of Department of Applied Marathi, linguistics and language teaching within the Arts faculty in all the universities of the state.
    - Empowering of Marathi language and literary associations in all colleges and university departments across Maharashtra.
    - Encouraging Universities in the state to actively engage in developing resources like dictionaries, lexicographical material etc.

- Developing time bound strategy to make Marathi the medium of instruction at the undergraduate and post graduate level in all disciplines.
- Reviving Vidyapeeth Granthnirmiti Mandal (Board for preparing texts for university level education.) that would prepare texts that would help in making Marathi, the language of advanced disciplines.
- Encouraging research in Marathi in all Disciplines.

• ***Section encouraging the use of Marathi in Central Government as well as private establishments***

- Establishment of a permanent mechanism for monitoring the usage of Marathi in these establishments.
- Enforcing the use of Marathi by penalising errant officials.
- Improving the quality of Marathi used in these establishments.

• ***Section looking after the use of Marathi in Judiciary***

- Training the bureaucrats in the Department of Law and Judiciary for drafting bills in Marathi.
- Developing infrastructure for conducting entire business of the lower judiciary in Marathi. That would include developing the Marathi version of 'The Case Information System' software prepared by National Informatics Centre, making available typists, stenos, computers, new staff, reference material etc.
- Undertaking efforts to make Marathi the authorised language of the High Court of Mumbai under Article 348(2) of the Constitution.
- Making available legal education in Marathi in all universities of Maharashtra.
- Conducting Examinations conducted of the Maharashtra Public Service Commission for the posts of civil judges

(junior division) and judicial magistrate (First class) simultaneously in Marathi.

- Incorporating a compulsory component of Marathi at various Judicial academies in Maharashtra in order to implement the June 1998 notification of the Government of Maharashtra, that makes Marathi the sole language of all district and taluka courts across Maharashtra.

- ***Section looking after learning Marathi language***
  - Creating an awareness among non-Maharashtrians in Maharashtra about the need to learn Marathi.
  - Making adequate reference material and teaching facilities available in a decentralised manner.
  - Making online and offline training and evaluation facilities available with the help of universities and civil society organisations.
  - Scientifically developed and technologically equipped courses of Marathi should be developed for Non-Marathi people should be developed. Such online and offline course would provide easy facilities for them to learn Marathi.

- ***Section looking after the use of Marathi in computers and information and communication technology***
  - Devising a time bound programme for the use of Unicode on in the entire business of Government of Maharashtra.
  - Establishing training facilities for the use of Unicode and inscript key board.
  - Spreading the use of bilingual key boards consisting of Marathi Devnagri and English in the state.[13]
  - Making it mandatory that every mobile sold in Marathi should have the in-built facility of using Marathi. Establishing appropriate mechanisms for ensuring compliance.

- Ensuring that all computers sold in Maharashtra have the Marathi Unicode action activated in them.[14]
- Ensuring that the E-governance modules of the Government of Maharashtra are implemented in Marathi as well. Ensuring that all the websites of the Government of Maharashtra are in Unicode Marathi using open source software. Coordinating with IIT, CDAC, and NIC regarding localisation of ICT in Marathi.
- Evolving machinery for training to the employees of Government of Maharashtra regarding Unicode and inscript. Making inscript based typing mandatory for all recruitments under the Government of Maharashtra.
- Enabling standardisation of fonts and keyboards fonts sold in Maharashtra.
- Developing Unicode based free and open sourced Marathi fonts.
- Following up the issue of improvements in the I- 386 folder that contains character map for Marathi Devnagari script with the Unicode Consortium and the Central Government. However, the state government has to pursue this matter with the Central Government.
- Instructing all computer-training institutes in Maharashtra to compulsorily introduce Unicode system and the inscript keyboard.
- Incorporating a compulsory component of Unicode and Inscript typing in MS- CIT exams conducted by Maharashtra Knowledge Corporation Limited (MKCL). Similarly, incorporating modules on Unicode and open source systems in school curricula.
- Undertaking time bound efforts for the development of Marathi Optical Character Recognition (OCR) system and Marathi spell checker.

   - Making classic books in Marathi that are free of copyright free books in Marathi available to people through the cyberspace with the participation of libraries and other institutions.[15]

- ***Section dealing with the employment for the Marathi youth***
   - Developing training modules that will give Marathi youth training of skills required for various jobs in the market.
   - Providing information to Marathi youth regarding vacancies in central, state and other establishments through the various field offices of Government of Maharashtra.
   - Creating agencies for training and counselling required for employment and self-employment, keeping in mind the fact that the number of Marathi youth opting for self-employment is comparatively less.
   - Under the Official Languages Act of the Government of India, states have been divided in categories like A, B, C. This categorisation is illogical and suits the interests of Hindi speaking states of North India while jeopardising the interests of Maharashtra. Maharashtra is included in B category and students from these categories are not given the option of mother tongue while answering various government level examinations. These provisions are thus detrimental to the interests of Maharashtra. Maharashtra Government should compel the Government of India to change these rules. If need be, legal recourse should be adopted.
   - Opening of district level information kiosks should be for giving employment-related information to the educated unemployed youth from rural Maharashtra.

- ***Section to look after Maharashtrians staying in other parts of India as well as in other countries of the world***
  - This group will connect with the Marathi Diaspora and the organisations working with them.
  - Through collaboration with foreign universities it will try to incorporate the teaching of Marathi in their syllabi. Such initiatives have already begun in some US universities.
  - Try to network with language related agencies in these states.
  - It will help the Marathi Diaspora develop library collections with the help of Directorate of Languages.

Besides these sections that will look into the development of Marathi language and culture, it is necessary to initiate action on the area of Centre - State relations. That would include pressurising the Union Government to appoint a new commission on the lines of the Sarkaria Commission to take a fresh look at the centre state relations in India and give wide ranging functional autonomy to states.

The structure and functions of the department mentioned above does not in itself provide a guarantee against bureaucratisation and governmental apathy. However, projecting a structure is essential because it gives us a structure within which we can operate.

The next question that needs to be addressed is: Is it possible to mobilise people for issues like language planning and development? What could be the nature of political organisation? As far as Maharashtra is concerned, we are familiar with two such mobilisations- one by Shivsena in the 1960s and the other by Maharashtra Navnirman Sena in 2006.[16] Although both these mobilisations have seen considerable support from the middle class Maharashtrians, as their election performance would reveal, they have not achieved their objectives beyond releasing the pent up anger of people. This is a sign of a much substantive flaw in the ideological premise of the parties: their failure to understand the linkage between language, culture and economic, political interests of a linguistic community.

The problems of language development and planning that we are discussing in the case of Maharashtra are not specific only to Maharashtra. Media reports about language problems in different states reveal that many problems faced by Indian languages are common. They only differ in intensity. For example, like Maharashtra even Karnataka, West Bengal, Assam have witnessed migration-related problems. Problems arising out of non-use of official languages in various domains of social life are seen in many parts of India. Developing a pan-Indian consensus on this issue is the key to mobilisation of people for their respective languages in a manner that has hitherto not been witnessed. It would attempt to bridge the gap between various linguistic communities and evolve a pan-Indian coalition of political parties. Such mobilisation on the basis of language issues would be constructive as it would attempt to Indian languages.

7.9 Social Movements and Language Movements

It is true that most social movements focus on the "Universal" rights of the people. Yet the issue of language may be closely linked with the issues they take. For example, if there is a court case over land acquisition in most such case, court proceedings in regional languages would become far more useful to the aggrieved people than proceedings in English. Unfortunately, this point is missed by both rights movements and language movements.

Raising the language issues as rights issues would not only strengthen social movements, it would also force contemporary language movements to change their outlook and be more proactive towards economic problems. This would eventually replace the notional and symbolic components of language-based identity movements by a more substantive economic and political agenda.

There is increasing awareness among linguists and activists on two issues: that it is not possible to protect Indian languages unless they are linked with the economic opportunities of its speakers and that it is possible to engage with globalisation using the very tools that it has created for e.g. ICT. To fulfill this aim Marathikaaran will need to focus on

- Proactive role of the state in language planning and development.
- Connectedness with progressive social movements, and
- Engaging with the forces of cultural globalisation.

This three-fold agenda would contribute to the evolution of Marathikaaran. A relevant question would be: Who would take up the mantle of this new politics? While it is not entirely impossible for present day mainstream parties to take up this task, looking at the ideological incongruencies there is limited efficacy in their ideological repositioning. Rather, a new political mobilisation based on this ideology may be a better option. Another Samyukta Maharashtra like movement may be needed to take up this responsibility. How this new identity movement will emerge and how it will change the politics of Maharashtra remains to be seen.

Notes and References

1. Throughout the industrial revolution and consequent colonialism and imperialism, English has been the vehicle of the western world especially Britain. Even in the latest phase of globalisation, multiple global level institutions have promoted English in an unprecedented manner. Without the active patronage of Governments and the Market, English would not have acquired the prominence that it has acquired in our times. For details see Phillipson, Robert: L*inguistic imperialism continued, Routledge* New York and London 2009. Also published in New Delhi, India in 2009 for seven South Asian countries by Orient Blackswan.

   And Phillipson, Robert, *Linguistic imperialism*. Oxford: Oxford University Press, 1992.

2. For details of the English only policies in the USA see http://www.linguapax.org/congres/taller/taller1/Beykont.html.

   For the details of Language planning in China see http://www.cal.org/heritage/pdfs/briefs/language-planning-in-china.pdf

   For the details of language planning in Indonesia see http://www.bcs.rochester.edu/cls/s2009v5n1/Paauw.pdf

For the details of Language planning in France and Denmark see http://www.immi.se/intercultural/nr3/bakmand.htm

For the details of Language planning in Africa See the Harare Declaration at http://ocpa.irmo.hr/resources/docs/Harare_Language-en.pdf

3. Government of Maharashtra, Gujarat, West Bengal, Assam to name a few.
4. For a theoretical analysis of Language planning with country wise explanation see Gadelii Karl Erland, *Language Planning: Theory and Practice Evaluation of language planning cases worldwide, Languages Division Education Sector UNESCO,1999. It can be accessed at* http://unesdoc.unesco.org/images/0011/001184/118456eo.pdf
5. India can be best described as a model of linguistic pluralism rather than assimilation. Although, the supporters of Hindi (in the early years after independence) and the supporters of English (after globalisation) have been arguing for the preeminence of their respective language in all domains of social life, their claim has not been universally accepted. However compared to Hindi, English has been more successful in usurping the spaces available for other languages. There are attempts by a section of the English media to propagate English language as the lingua franca of the elites, but these efforts have met with stiff resistance.
6. Kaplan, B., Robert, and Richard B. Baldauf Jr. *Language Planning from Practice to Theory.* Clevedon: Multilingual Matters ltd., 1997.
7. For details of certain countries' language policy features see http://www.seameo.org/vl/Language0607.pdf
8. There are many ways in which language policies can be categorized. It was elaborated by Université Laval sociolinguist Jacques Leclerc for the French-language Web site L'aménagement linguistique dans le monde put on line by the CIRAL in 1999. The collecting, translating and classifying of language policies started in 1988 and culminated in the publishing of Recueil des législations linguistiques dans le monde (Vol. I to VI) at Presses de l'Université Laval in 1994. The work, containing some 470 language laws, and the research leading to publication, were subsidized by the Office Québécois de la langue française. [1] In April 2008, the Web site presented the linguistic portrait and language policies in 354 States or autonomous territories in 194 recognised countries.
9. For details of the Universal Declaration on Linguistic Rights see http://www.unesco.org/cpp/uk/declarations/linguistic.pdf
10. Bòrd na Gàidhlig, Dutch Language Union, Foras na Gaeilge, Office Québécois de la langue française, Welsh Language Board, Pan South African Language Board are some of the language regulators that look after the development and promotion in their respective countries.
11. Details about the Bòrd na Gàidhlig can be accessed at http://www.gaidhlig.org.uk/bord/en

12. Details about the Dutch Language Union and The Netharlandse Taalunie can be accessed at http://taalunieversum.org/en/
13. This has been initiated by the Department of Information Technology, Government of India for all languages. Even the Government of Maharashtra had purchased bilingual keyboards in bulk amount. However, in the absence of a directive to promote Unicode and Inscript and unavailability of training mechanism, the whole exercise turned futile. For more details on the Inscript keyboard see http://tdil.mit.gov.in/pdf/keyboard/Keyboardper cent20 Standard.pdf
14. Corporate companies are looking at localisation positively as a business opportunity. This researcher had an opportunity to interact with Meghashyam Karnam, Localisation head of Microsoft (India). He and his team were willing to make the Unicode option available provided the Government of Maharashtra instructs them to do so. Meeting on 22.02.10 at the Microsoft Office Mumbai.
15. One such effort is undertaken by the Esamvad team. For details please see http://www.marathipustake.org/Index.html
16. That also explains the changing locus of competition from the formal sector to the informal sector. That can be attributed to the changing economic scenario ushered in by globalisation.

Chapter 8

Summary and Conclusions

8.1 Introducing Language Politics

Language politics as identity-based politics has been a subject of major political concern in India post-independence. Real or perceived injustice to a linguistic community has also been a major concern. Similarly, the ways and means of making the use of official languages of the states in various domains of social life has also been a matter of intense debate. Problems of identity politics based on language that India has encountered are not unique to the country. The review of Constitutional Provisions on language as presented above sets the tone for understanding the complexities of the politics of language.

8.2 Constitutional Provisions

The Indian Constitution guarantees the status of minority languages. However, it does not have explicit provisions for the protection of majority languages that have become official languages of various linguistic states after they were created. The reason may be that the Congress leadership involved in the making of the Constitution had not visualised that the demands for creation of linguistic states would be so widespread and mass-based across India. Elaborate mechanisms of language planning may not guarantee the development of a language, yet it would create conducive atmosphere for the various stakeholders in language development to proactively engage with the issue. This however can simplify the need for language planning for the language of the majority and the official language of a state.

8.3 Samyukta Maharashtra Movement

The movement for the creation of Unified or Samyukta Maharashtra is a major event not only in the history of Maharashtra, but also in the post-independent history of India. As a movement it drew attention of people across the country. There were many hurdles to the creation of Unified Maharashtra. They were:

- The inclusion of the city of Bombay in Maharashtra.
- The dissolution of Nizam's Hyderabad state and the inclusion of Marathi speaking areas of Marathwada in Maharashtra.
- Negotiations with the leadership of Vidarbha so that some of them demanding for Separate Mahavidarbha state give up that demand and join Maharashtra.
- Inclusion of Goa in Maharashtra after its liberation.
- Inclusion of the border areas of Belgaum, Karwar, Nipani, Khanapur, Bidar, Bhalki, Supa, Halyal in Maharashtra by settling the dispute with the state of Mysore.
- Including the Dangs district bordering Gujarat in Maharashtra, since Dangi was a dialect of Marathi.

The protracted struggle led by the Samyukta Maharashtra Samiti was able to achieve unified Maharashtra. Almost five decades after the existence of the Movement, it is appropriate to evaluate its performance. The Samiti was a fragile coalition working under mass pressure. It remarkably made use of the independent Media for promoting the struggle. Participation of the cultural representatives of the subaltern class like Shahirs and other folk singers was quite impressive. Participation of Non-Maharashtrians and condemnation of violence gave legitimacy to the movement. The role of Congress and Yashwantrao Chavan during the movement was far from satisfactory. Only when it became clear that the Congress would lose elections in 1962 that the Congress decided to break the bigger bilingual state.

Although the Samiti leadership had talked about the development of Marathi language and culture and employment issues of the Marathi speaking people, they could not evolve a comprehensive agenda for the same. Although the Samyukta Maharashtra Samiti mobilised masses for the creation of Samyukta Maharashtra with Bombay as its capital, it did not spend much of energy on developing a comprehensive agenda for the development of Marathi language, culture and the empowerment of the Marathi speaking people after the creation of Maharashtra. Had the Samiti sustained as a political force, it is quite possible that the language and culture scene in Maharashtra would have been different.

8.4 Chavan and the Congress's Role in Language Development

After taking over the responsibility as the Chief Minister of Unified Maharashtra, Yashwantrao Chavan spelled out his vision about the development of the state and development of the Marathi language. He also expressed the need to run the administration of Maharashtra in Marathi language instead of English. Immediately after the creation of the state, Chavan established the following language, literature and culture related bodies.

- Bhasha Sanchalanalay (Directorate of languages).
- Sahitya ani Sanskruti Mandal (Board for literature and Culture).
- Vishwakosh Nirmiti Mandal (Board for Marathi Encyclopedia).
- Vidyapeeth Grantha Nirmiti Mandal (Board for creation of university level reference books).

The Maharashtra Official Languages Act 1964 was passed in 1965. The responsibility to implement this as well as to enhance the use of Marathi in administration was entrusted with the

Directorate of Languages by this Act. A Language Advisory Committee was established to aid and advice the government about the enhanced use of Marathi in the administration.

This detailed review of government efforts makes it strikingly clear as to *Why it did not work.*

- The State government had never set any deadline for transacting the entire business of the administration in Marathi. Although there is mention of the 1985 deadline, it was more notional than realistic.
- The political elite does not seem to be committed to running the business of the government in Marathi, this despite the fact that majority of the members of the legislature were from rural Maharashtra where Marathi was the lingua franca of the people.
- Except very late, there was no mention of any punitive action against errant bureaucrats. Thus, there was no fear of punishment to those who defaulted.
- The Congress leadership including Yashwantrao Chavan who was quite an influential politician of the state until the early 1980s had not publicly criticized the bureaucracy for non-compliance, which meant that no one was in a hurry about the use of Marathi in administration. Ravishankar Shukla, the Chief Minister of the erstwhile Central provinces had refused to sign on files where notes were written in English. Had a similar approach been applied by the political leadership in Maharashtra, the use of Marathi in administration would have been quite impressive.

A close overview of the functioning of Maharashtra Government's language and literary agencies gives us the feeling that the state is both inefficient and indifferent towards language-related issues. The state government has paid notional tribute to its official language.

8.5 Shivsena and Language Politics

Shivsena was formed in 1966 by Bal Thackeray and some of his associates to fight against the perceived injustice against the Marathi speaking people in Maharashtra especially in the city of Bombay. The emergence of Shivsena was not a sudden development. The declining importance of Maharashtrians in the political economy of the city of Mumbai was a matter of serious concern much before the arrival of Shivsena. Besides the issue of employment to Marathi youth, Shivsena has undertaken various activities through which it tried to mobilise the Marathi Manoos and became a political force to reckon with. For that it established more than a dozen allied organisations. Some of the key campaigns of the Shivsena were:

- Struggle for the disputed border areas of Belgaum, Karwar, Nipani and Bidar etc.
- Marathi signboards on shops and other establishments.
- Renaming the city of Bombay as Mumbai.
- Use of Marathi in the business of the Government.
- Use of Marathi in the Judiciary.

Within the limits of its political strength, Shivsena tried to pressurise the government about the use of Marathi. However, throughout its political life spanning 45 years, Shivsena has never attempted to prepare a strategic note or action plan about the enhanced use of Marathi in administration. Shivsena made a shift of emphasis from Marathi Manoos to Hindujan during the 1980s. Post-1985 Shivsena has neither been truly Hindu nor truly Maharashtrian. However, in the absence of a parallel organisation that could expose the limitations of Shivsena, the latter still monopolised the Marathi agenda.

8.6 MNS and Language Politics

MNS was formed in 2006 by Raj Thackeray. Its formation was a result of a struggle between Raj and Uddhav Thackeray over leadership and the subsequent breaking away of Raj from Shivsena. The vision statement of the party is an important document to look into the mind of its leadership. The definition of Marathi Manoos includes even those people who are born in the state not to Marathi parents but who speak Marathi. Another interesting factor is the collaboration of constructive and street politics MNS has taken up the following issues:

- Control the political dominance of migrants and protect the opportunities of the Marathi Manoos.
- Make teaching of Marathi language compulsory in all schools in Maharashtra.
- Insist on Marathi language and Marathi sign-boards everywhere.
- On the Disputed border areas.

Besides the Shivsena and the MNS, other political parties have not built their politics on the Nativist agenda.

8.7 Civil Society Organisations

Besides political parties, various civil society organisations have also been working on the issues of Marathi language and culture. Maharashtra has a strong presence of civil society organisations. Literary agencies like Sahitya Parishads are supposed to look after the development of Marathi language. One of the major problems created by the way our literary agencies are handled is that confusion of the political leaders as well as literary figures about issues of literary development and issues of language development has further deepened. All these organisations have used various instruments to pursue their agenda. Some of them are as follows:

- Writing letters, petitions to the government, semi-government authorities.
- Collaborating with like-minded organisations to pursue a matter and sensitise people over language issues.
- Seeking information under the Right to Information about the use or non-use of Marathi in various domains and using this information as a tool for campaigning.

- Lobbying with political parties and their students units, trade unions wings and providing them inputs on the basis of which parties can make language policies.
- Advocacy in the legislature, raise questions through individual MLAs who may show interest on certain issues either due to taking up of these issues by the media or to take the ruling parties to task.
- Proactive use of the media.

8.8 Advantages and Disadvantages of CSOs

There are various advantages and disadvantages of these instruments. Advantages are as follows:

I. If one campaign using a certain instrument gets success, the same instrument may be used by others thus increasing the pace of activism.

II. Some of these groups have been recognised as pressure groups on language issues. Opinions of such organisations are taken into consideration during media debates or while drafting manifestos of political parties.

III. Success with one agency may mean that other similar agencies follow suit. E.g. one mobile operator makes the Marathi option available in the IVR (Interactive Voice Response) system, other mobile operators may follow suit. However, one should be warned against idealism because the corporate sector is generally apathetic to local languages.

IV. Such campaigns require minimum human and material resources. With the spread of information and communication technology, campaigning and canvassing has become less expensive. Thus, a sustained campaign can achieve visible results with minimum resources and it can open the field for many such smaller, local and low cost initiatives.

However, such initiatives also have limitations;

- Organisations with limited resources can take up only one issue at a time. Thus, the number of issues addressed at a time would be very less.

- Deciding procedures for activism remains voluntary. Under these circumstances, professional strategising may be lacking in such organisations.
- Various initiatives may get symbolic or occasionally even real success but penetrating the political system and bringing about macro policy changes sometimes becomes difficult.
- Civil society organisations have an option to join a political party and carry their agenda forward. However, that may compromise their autonomy. More importantly, the perspective of mainstream political parties working for Marathi language and the approach of many civil society organisations is not similar. More so, civil society organisations do not have a common platform to strengthen themselves and avoid duplication of work. Thus, civil society organisations are caught between the devil and the deep sea. Efforts have been made by Marathi Abhyas Kendra and Marathi Ekjoot to bring together civil society activists working for Marathi language. However, these efforts have not borne fruit.

8.9 Marathikaaran- New Politics of Marathi

Language is essentially a political issue and therefore it has to be suitably handled through a language-based political movement. Such a movement has to develop a linkage between Marathi language, culture and economic interests of the Marathi speaking people. Henceforth, this ideology would be described as 'Marathikaaran' – Politics and the movement of Marathikaaran will have to aim at:

- Implementation of constitutional provisions regarding the empowerment of Indian languages (in this case the empowerment of Marathi).
- Implementation of various provisions regarding the development of Marathi that have been enacted since the creation of Unified Maharashtra.

- Developing suitable institutional mechanisms for the promotion of Marathi language and culture.
- Enhancing the collaboration between the Government and Non-Government institutions for developing a comprehensive plan for the development of Marathi language and culture.
- Evolving a constructive, substantive framework for the development of Marathi language and culture which can facilitate the emergence of a mass movement that is not merely reactive and symbolic in nature.
- Ensuring that this movement categorically avoids recourse to violence.
- Preserving the linguistic rights of minorities while ensuring the rights of Majority Maharashtrians.

While it is true that mere state initiative or intervention can't ensure the development of a language, it must be noted that nowhere in the contemporary world have languages survived or flourished without state help. Unfortunately in India, the issue has not been given as much importance as it deserves. After the linguistic reorganisation of states (the process that continued till the 1970s), various states did undertake initiatives for the development of their respective official languages. However, there was a huge gap between the pace of legislation and the requirements of Language planning. As far as Maharashtra is concerned, the use of Marathi in state administration, judiciary, education and technology still remained a distant goal.

8.10 Language Policy and Language Planning

Many countries or regions within a country have a language policy designed to favour or discourage the use of a particular language or set of languages. Although nations historically have used language policies most often to promote one official language at the expense of others, many countries now have policies designed to protect and promote regional and ethnic languages whose viability is threatened. Language policy is what a government does either officially through legislation, court decisions or policy to determine how languages are used to cultivate language skills needed to meet national priorities or to establish the rights of individuals or groups to use and maintain languages.

The establishment of a separate department for the development of Marathi Language within the Government of Maharashtra has begun the process of language planning. However, the department needs to be more broad-based in its structure and functions. To develop Marathi language as a social resource (like land, water and energy) and to establish a permanent, transparent and accountable agency for the development of Marathi would be the objective of the Department if it is to be an effective language regulator.

8.11 Proposed Structure of the Department of Marathi Language

Besides the present literary agencies, the Department of Marathi would include following sub-units:

- Section working on Marathi as medium of instruction and the expansion of Marathi education.
- Section encouraging the use of Marathi in Central Government as well as private establishments.
- Section looking after the use of Marathi in Judiciary.
- Section looking after learning Marathi language.
- Section looking after the use of Marathi in computers and information and communication technology.
- Section dealing with the employment for the Marathi youth.
- Section to look after Maharashtrians staying in other parts of India as well as in other countries of the world.

The structure and functions of the department mentioned above do not in itself provide a guarantee against bureaucratisation and governmental apathy. However, projecting a structure is essential because it gives us a structure within which we can operate. The problems of language development and planning that we are discussing in the case of Maharashtra are not specific only to Maharashtra. Media reports about language problems in different states reveal that many problems faced by Indian languages are common. They only differ in intensity.

8.12 Conclusion

There is increasing awareness among linguists and activists on two issues: that it is not possible to protect Indian languages unless they are linked with the economic opportunities of its speakers and that it is possible to engage with globalisation using the very tools that it has creater. For example, ICT. To fulfill this aim Marathikaaran will need to focus on

- Proactive role of the state in language planning and development.
- Connectedness with progressive social movements, and
- Engaging with the forces of cultural globalisation.

How this new identity movement will emerge and how it will change the politics of Maharashtra remains to be seen.

Bibliography

Constituent Assembly Debates

http://parliamentofindia.nic.in/ls/debates/debates.htm

Official websites of Union Government and Maharashtra State Government

http://www.languageinindia.com/april2002/officiallanguages act.html

The full and updated text of the Constitution of India can be found at

http://lawmin.nic.in/

http://indiacode.nic.in/coiweb/welcome.html

http://socialjustice.nic.in/olact1963.php

http://rajbhasha.nic.in/

http://rajbhashasamiti.gov.in/

http://capart.nic.in

Other websites

http://www.tariqrahman.net/language/Roleper cent20of per cent20Englishper cent20inper cent20Pakistan.htm

http://www.terralingua.org/

http://www.ambedkar.org/

http://bhasha.maharashtra.gov.in

http://www.gms.maharashtra.gov.in/bhasha/Prashasanik LekhanKosh.aspx

http://mahasahityasanskruti.maharashtra.gov.in

http://vishwakosh.org.in

http://rmvs.maharashtra.gov.in

www.manase.org

http://web.worldbank.org

http://www.constitution.org

http://www.marxists.org

http://www.maharashtra.ngosindia.com

http://mr.upakram.org

http://amrutmanthan.wordpress.com

http://unicode.org/

http://www.linguapax.org/congres/taller/taller1/Beykont.html

http://www.cal.org/heritage/pdfs/briefs/language-planning-in-china.pdf

http://www.bcs.rochester.edu/cls/s2009v5n1/Paauw.pdf

http://www.immi.se/intercultural/nr3/bakmand.htm

http://ocpa.irmo.hr/resources/docs/Harare_Language-en.pdf

http://unesdoc.unesco.org/

http://www.seameo.org/

http://www.gaidhlig.org.uk/

http://taalunieversum.org/

http://tdil.mit.gov.in

http://www.marathipustake.org/

http://plato.stanford.edu/

http://bitbucket.icaap.org/

Journals, Periodicals, Yearbooks and Newspapers

- **Seminar**
- **Sadhana**
- **Economic and Political Weekly**
- **Samaj Prabodhan Patrika**
- **Anubhav**

- **Navbharat**
- **Bhasha Ani Jeevan**
- **Ruchi**
- **The Marxist**
- **Kalnirnay Sanskrutik**
- **Marmik**
- **Loksatta**
- **Saamna**
- **Maharashtra Times**
- **Sakal**
- **Prahaar**
- **Hindu**
- **India Today**
- **DNA**
- **Indian Express**
- **Hindustan Times**

Manifestos of Political Parties

The Election Manifesto of the CPI (M)

The CPI election manifesto

Election manifesto of the Socialist Party

The Bharatiya Jan Sangh Election Manifesto

Books

1. *Abhyaskramat Mahiti Tantradnyan- Shasanachi Bhumika*- Shaleya Shikshan Vibhag, Maharashtra Shasan, Mumbai, January 2002.
2. Adarkar, Neera and Menon, Meena- *Katha Mumbaichya Girangaochi*, (Mauj Prakashan, Mumbai, 2007).
3. Aiyar, S P – *Federalism and Social Change: A Study in Quasi Federalism* (1961, Asia Publishing House, Bombay).

4. Akolkar, Prakash, *Jai Maharashtra, Ha Shivsena Navacha Itihas ahe* (Mumbai, Prabhat Prakashan, 1998).
5. Anderson, Benedict, *Imagined Communities: Reflections on the Origin and Spread of Nationalism.* (Revised Edition ed. London and New York: Verso, 1991, pp. 5-7).
6. Annamalai, E (Ed), *Language Movements in India* – (1979, Central Institute of Indian Languages, Manas Gangotri).
7. Austin, Granville, *Working a democratic constitution: The Indian experience*; (OUP, Fifth impression, 2001).
8. Azam, Kausar J, *Federalism and Good Governance: Issues Across Culture* (1998, South Asian Publishers, New Delhi).
9. Bagle, Prabhakar (Ed.), *Haddaparichya Waatewaril Marathi*- Anushtubh Pratishthan, Mumbai, January, 2002.
10. Basu, Amruta and Kohli Atul (Ed.), *Community Conflicts and the State in India* – (OUP, 1998).
11. Baylis, John, Smith Steve, *The Globalisation of World Politics*, (OUP, 2005).
12. Beard, Adrian, *Language of Politics* (2000, Routledge London).
13. Bedekar, D.K., *Samyukta Maharashtra*, (Chitrashala Prakashan, Pune 1947).
14. Bhalerao, Nishikant (Ed), *Samagra Anant Bhalerao*, Vol. I, 2nd edition, (Darpan Pratishthan Nanded, July 2011, p. 320).
15. Bhatia, K L, *Federalism and Frictions in Centre-State Relations: A Comparative Review of Indian and German Constitutions* (2001, Deep & Deep, New Delhi).
16. Bloom, Paul, Peterson Mary A, Nadel Lynn, Garett Merill F (Ed.), *Language and Space* (1999, Cambridge, MIT).
17. Bourdieu, Pierre, *The Logic of Practice*, (Stanford University Press, Stanford California 1990).
18. Brass, Paul, *Ethnicity and Nationalism, Theory and Comparison*, (Sage Publications, 1991) p.18.

19. Census 1991, *Language Atlas of India* (2004, Delhi, Controller of Publications).
20. Chandra, Bipin et. al. (ed.), *India after independence 1947-2000* (Penguin books, 2000).
21. Chausalkar, Ashok, *Comrade Shreepad Amrut Dange*, (Comrade Govind Pansare Amrut Mahotsav Samiti Prakashan, Kolhapur, May 2011, pp. 290-292).
22. Chavan, Yashwantrao, *Sahyadriche Ware, Mukhyamantri Yashwantrao Chavan Yanchya Nivdak Bhashnancha Sangraha*- (Yashwantrao Chavan Pratishthan, Mumbai, Third Edition, 1992).
23. Copland, Ian, Rickard John (Ed), *Federalism: Comparative Perspectives from India and Australia* (Monash University, National Centre for Australian Studies).
24. Coupland, Nikolas- *The Handbook of Language and globalisation*- (Wiley-Blackwell, 2010).
25. Dange, S.A., *Bara Bhashane*, (Abhinav Prakashan, Mumbai, January 1967).
26. David, Crystal – *Language Death* (2000, Cambridge, Cambridge University Press).
27. Deo, Shankarrao, *Daiva Dete Pan Karma Nete* (Saswad Ashram Vishwasta Mandal Publication, Pune 1976).
28. Dharmadhikari, Bhau (Ed), *Gandhi Vichardarshan,* Vol.1, Maharashtra Gandhi Smarak Nidhi Prakashan, 3rd Edition, May 1995, pp. 130-132.
29. Downes, William – *Language and Society* (London, Fontana).
30. Downing, John; Ali Mohammadi, Annabelle Sreberny-Mohammadi (1995), *Questioning the media: a critical introduction* (2, illustrated Ed.). SAGE. p. 482.
31. Dua, Hans R, *Language Planning in India* (1985, Harnam Publications, New Delhi).
32. Fishman, Joshua A – (Ed), *Language Problems of Developing*

Nations (1968, New York, John Wiley).

33. Gadgil, B.Y., *Haak Swayatta Maharashtrachi*, 2nd edition, Granthali,1999.
34. Gadgil, D R, *Federal Problem in India* (1947, Poona).
35. Ghosh, Partha S., *Ethnicity versus Nationalism* – The Devolution discourse in Sri Lanka, Sage Publication, New Delhi, 2003.
36. Giddens, Anthony, *The Consequences of Modernity* (Cambridge: Polity, 1990).
37. Gilpin, Robert, *Global Political Economy: Understanding the International Economic Order* (Princeton University Press, 2001).
38. Gokhale, D.N., *Dr Ketkar* (2nd edition, Majestic publication, Mumbai, 1981).
39. Goswami, Sandhya, *Language Politics in Assam* (1997, Ajanta Publications, New Delhi).
40. Gupta, Dipankar, *Nativism in a metropolis: Shivsena in Bombay*, (Mumbai, Manohar, 1982).
41. Gupta, Jyotirindra Das - *Language Conflict and National Development: Group Politics and National Language Policy in India* (University of California Press, 1970).
42. Haksar, K N, Panikkar K M, *Federal India* (1930, Martin Hopkinson, London).
43. Hansen, Thomas Blom – *Urban violence in India: Identity politics, Mumbai and the postcolonial city*, (Permanent black, 2001).
44. Harris, Roxy, Rampton Ben (Ed), *Language Ethnicity and Race Reader* (2003, Routledge London).
45. Joshi, Manohar, *Shivsena – Kaal, Aaj, Udya - History of Shivsena from 1966*, (Mumbai, Prabodhan Prakashan, 2008).
46. Joshi, Manohar, *Shivsenechi Nirmiti, Waadh, Swarup, Yashapayash ani Bhartiya Rajkarnatil Shivseneche Bhavitavya Yacha Vishleshanatmak Abhyas* (Analytical study

of the emergence, growth, nature, success and failure and future in national politics of Shivsena) (University of Mumbai, Rajiv Gandhi Centre for Contemporary Studies, 2009).

47. Katzenstein, Mary Fainsod, *Ethnicity and Equality: The Shiv Sena Party and Preferential Policies in Bombay* (Cornell University Press, 1979).
48. Kelekar, Ravindra, *Bhashik Sangharshache Samajshastra*, (Rajhans Prakashan, Panaji, 2008).
49. Kelkar, Indumati, *Lohia*, (National Book Trust, 1983).
50. Khemani, Stuti, *Federal Politics and Budget Deficits: Evidence from the States in India* (2002, World Bank, Washington D.C.).
51. Khubchandani, Lachman M (Ed), *Language in a Plural Society* (1988, Motilal Banarasidas, Delhi).
52. King, Robert D, *Nehru and the Language Politics of India* (1997, OUP).
53. Kramarae Cheris, Schutz Mureil, O'barr William M, *Language and Power* (1984, London, Sage).
54. Kramsch, Claire, *Language and Culture* (2001, OUP Delhi).
55. Kymlicka, Will, *Multicultural Citizenship: A Liberal Theory of Minority Rights* (Oxford: Oxford University Press, 1995).
56. Lee, Siu-Nam Lee (1988), *"Communication imperialism and dependency: A conceptual clarification"*, International Communication Gazette (Netherlands: Kiuwer Academic Publishers) (41): 74.
57. Lele, R.K., *Marathi Vruttapatrancha Itihas*, (Continental Prakashan, Pune, Third edition).
58. Mahajan, Gurpreet – *Identities and Rights: Aspects of Liberal Democracy* (2001, OUP, Delhi).
59. *Maharashtra Rajbhasha Adhiniyam, 1964 wa tyakhalil niyam ani adesh ityadinchya sankalanachi puravani pustika (compilation of rules from Jan.1988 to July 1993)*, Shasakiy Madhyavarti Mudranalay, Mumbai, 1996.

60. *Maharashtra Rajbhasha adhiniyam, 1964 wa tyakhalil niyam ani adesh ityadinchya sankalanachi pustika (compilation of rules upto December 1987)*, Shasakiy Madhyavarti Mudranalay, Mumbai, 1988.

61. *Maharashtra Rajya Sahitya Ani Sanskruti Mandal: Sadhan ani Sadhya*, Maharashtra Rajya Sahitya Ani Sanskruti Mandal Prakashan, October 2010.

62. *Maharashtra Universities Act 1994*, Principal, Dr Shivajirao S. Kadam & others, Hind Law House, 2001, p. 91.

63. Majeed, Akhtar (Ed), *Federalism without the Union: A Distribution of Responsibilities in the Indian System* (2004, Centre for Federal Studies, New Delhi).

64. Manjali, Franson D (Ed), *Language, Society & Discourse* (1992, Bahri Publications, New Delhi).

65. Marathi encyclopedia : Marathi Vishvakosh- Khandal.

66. *Marathicha Jahirnama*, Marathi Abhyas Kendra Publication, 2009.

67. Mathkar, Jayanand, *Maharashtrache Shilpakar Barrister Nath Pai*, (Maharashtra Rajya Sahitya Sanskruti Mandal Prakashan, Mumbai, 2nd Edition, September 2008).

68. McPhail, Thomas L. (1987), *Electronic colonialism: the future of international broadcasting and communication,* Volume 126 of Sage library of social research. Sage Publications, p. 18.

69. More, Sadanand, *Lokmanya te Mahatma,* Vol.1 and 2 (Rajhans Prakashan, Pune, 2007).

70. Morris, Jacques, Morris Michael (Ed), *Language in Globalizing World* (2003, Cambridge, Cambridge University Press).

71. Mukherjee, Nirmal, Arora Balveer (Ed), *Federalism in India: Origins and Development* (1992, Vikas Publishing House, New Delhi).

72. Nahir, Moshe, *Language Planning Goals: A classification* (First published in 1984) Republished in Christina B.

73. Naregal, Veena, *Language Politics, Elites & Pub. Sphere* (2001, Permanent Black, New Delhi).
74. *Nondi- Vidhimandalatil Nivadak Bhashane* - (Maharashtra Vidhanbhavan Amrutmahotsav Samiti, Mumbai, 2011).
75. *Nyayalayin Vyavahar ani Marathi Bhasha*, Yashwantrao Chavan Pratishthan, Mumbai, 1st edition, March 2007.
76. Palshikar, Suhas and Kulkarni Suhas (Ed.), *Maharashtratil Sattasangharsha Rajakiy Pakshanchi waatchal*, Samakalin Prakashan, 2007, Samakalin Prakashan.
77. Parekh, Bhikhu, *Rethinking Multiculturalism:. Cultural Diversity and Political Theory*, Harvard, UP. 2002.
78. Paulston and Richard Tucker, eds., *Sociolinguistics: The Essential Readings*, pp. 423-448. (Oxford: Blackwell, 2003).
79. Pawar, Datta, *Marathi Bhasha:Apeksha ani Upeksha*, Sahityasanwad Prakashan, Mumbai, December, 1996.
80. Pendse, Lalji, *Maharashtrache Mahamanthan*, 2nd edition, (Mumbai, Lokwangmay Griha, May 2010).
81. Phadke, Dr Y.D., *Politics and language*: (Himalaya Publishing House, Mumbai, 1979).
82. Phadke, Y.D., *Visavya Shtakatil Maharashtra,* Vols. VI,VII, VIII (Mauj Prakashan, Mumbai, 2007).
83. Phillipson, Robert, *Linguistic Imperialism, 1992 & Linguistic imperialism continued* (Orient Black Swan, 2009).
84. Potdar, Datto Waman – *Shroteho (A collection of speeches by Datto Waman Potdar),* (Venus Book stall, Pune, 1959, pp. 57-87).
85. Pradhan, G. P. and Jadhav, R G (Ed.) *Nivadak Sadhana* Vol.1, (Sadhana Prakashan, Pune, 2007).
86. Principal, Kadam Dr Shivajirao S. & others, *Maharashtra Universities Act 1994*, (Hind Law House 2001).
87. Purandare, Vaibhav, *The Sena Story* –(Mumbai Business Publications Inc, 1999).

88. Rahman, Tariq, *Language and Politics in Pakistan*: (Orient Longman, 2007).

89. Rahman, Tariq – *Language Ideology and power – Language learning among the Muslims of Pakistan and North India*, (Orient Longman, 2000).

90. Reddi, G Sunanda - *Language Problem in India* (1973, National Building House, Delhi).

91. Riggins, Stephen Harold (Ed.), *Language and Politics of Exclusion: Others in Discovery* (1997, Thousand Oaks, Sage).

92. Romaine, Suzanne, *Language in Society: An Introduction to Sociolinguistics* (1994, OUP).

93. Roy, Ramashray (Ed), *Federal Experience: India and Russia* – (2003, ICSSR New Delhi, Shipra).

94. Saez Lawrence, *Federalism without a Centre: The Impact of Political and Economic Reforms on India's Federal System* (2002, Sage Publications, New Delhi).

95. Sahasrabuddhe, P.G., *Maharashtra Sanskruti,* 4th edition (Continental Prakashan, Pune, 2011).

96. Sarangee, Asha, *Language and Politics in India*, (OUP, New Delhi, 2009, p. 43).

97. Sawer, Geoffrey (Ed) – *Federalism, an Australian Jubilee Study* (1952, Australian National University, Melbourne, F W Cheshire).

98. Scholte, Jan Aart, *Globalisation : A Critical Introduction* (London, Macmillan, 2000).

99. Shapiro, Michael J. (Ed.), *Language and Politics* (1984, Oxford, Basil Blackwell).

100. *Shasanvyavaharat Marathi: Samasya, Swarup, Prakriya, Bhasha Sanchalanalay, Maharashtra Shasan*, (year of publication not given)

101. Shejwalkar, T.S., *Panipat 1761* (7th edition, Rajhans Prakashan, Pune 2011) and Shejwalkar T.S, *Nivdak Lekhsangraha* - (Ha.Vi. Mote Prakashan, Mumbai, 1977).

102. Shewalkar, Ram (Ed.), *Lokmanya Tilakanche Nibandh*, (National Book Trust, New Delhi, 1996).

103. Smith, Graham (Ed) – *Federalism: The Multi-Ethnic Challenge* (1995, Longman, London).

104. Smith, Anthony D, *The Ethnic Origins of Nations,* (Blackwell, 1987).

105. Spolsky, Bernard, *Language Policy: Key issues in sociolinguistics*, (Cambridge University Press, 2004).

106. Talwalkar, Govind, *Yashwantrao: Vyaktitva ani Kartrutva*, (Yashwantrao Chavan Pratishthan, Mumbai, April 2012, p. 73).

107. Tendulkar, D.G. *Mahatama – Life of Mohandas Karamchand Gandhi,* Vol. I, (Publications Division, New Delhi, December 1988).

108. Thomas Linda, Wareing Shan, *Language Society and Power: An Introduction,* (2000, Routledge, London).

109. Varshney, Ashutosh, *Ethnic Conflict and Civic Life: Hindus and Muslims in India*, (Yale University Press, 2002 and 2003).

110. Vora Rajendra, Palshikar Suhas – *Maharashtratil Sattantar* (Granthali, Mumbai, 1996).

Synopsis

Introduction

Language politics as identity-based politics has been a subject of academic as well as political concern in India post-independence. Language played a major role in the reorganisation of the states. During and after the linguistic re-organisation of states, doubts were raised about its impact on the unity and integrity of the country. Real or perceived injustice to a linguistic community has been a cause of political turmoil since then. Similarly, the ways and means of making the use of official languages of the states in various domains of social life has also been a matter of debate. The failure of respective State Governments in delivering in this regard has contributed to the emergence of civil society movements for the preservation of various languages and cultures across the country. With the onslaught of globalisation, linguistic identities are facing a severe challenge of survival. The issue of language and culture preservation and empowerment of linguistic communities has become complex. On this backdrop, I intend to study this subject.

Problems of identity politics based on language are not unique to India. Sri Lanka and Pakistan have faced similar problems. Tariq Rahman has analysed the language and politics interface in Pakistan. He has discussed the conflict between Urdu and other provincial languages in Pakistan for survival and supremacy and points our attention to the role of the political elite in use or non-use of a language. He raises the crucial point that language development or promotion is a part of the political process. Partha Ghosh's account of ethnic politics in Sri Lanka discusses the Tamil versus Sinhala controversy that led to the demands of secession. One of the major impediments in the resolution of conflict in Pakistan as well as Sri Lanka was the failure in reorganisation of states and consequent devolution of power. This comparison gives us an understanding that the linguistic reorganisation of states in India helped in diffusing tension between linguistic communities.

The issues related to cultural globalisation and consequent linguistic and cultural hegemonies have received the attention of academia and policy-makers quite late. Robert Phillipson has discussed how English language has become the tool of cultural globalisation and a new form of imperialism. He explains the ideology and economics behind the expansion of the English language and how it threatens the future of other languages in the world. There are others like Salikoko S. Mufwene who argue that this kind of generalisation perpetuates the myth of English as a killer language which is far from reality.

One of the major contemporary concerns has been the use of information and communication technology for the spread of a language. Language issues have enmeshed with technology and therefore it is difficult to study them in isolation. Debates on localisation as the tool of empowerment of languages follow. Production of software technologies in a particular language and consequent hegemonising has been discussed by many.

Hypothesis and research questions:

On this backdrop, I pose the following questions for research:

- What is the relationship between language as a marker of identity and the politics that uses language as an instrument?
- What are the various ways of mobilisation to foster linguistic identities?
- What role the state does or should play in promotion of a language in various domains of social life?

- What is the impact of globalisation on identities in general and linguistic identities in particular?
- What are the possible ways in which linguistic identities will be restructured by globalisation and consequent Information and Communication Technology revolution?

The present research aims at answering these and some other questions in the context of Maharashtra. The present study aims at studying the impact of the formation of Maharashtra State, Political parties engaged in mobilisation on the basis of Marathi language and civil society organisations working for the promotion of Marathi in various domains on the status of Marathi language, its development and use at various levels. It also tries to understand the impact of the forces of globalisation on identity formation and identity politics based on language, in Maharashtra.

This research seeks to answer the following issues:

1. Politics of Marathi linguistic identity has been an instrument of achieving political ends; and does *not necessarily* result in the protection, upliftment, development, and wider use of Marathi language.
2. With the onslaught of globalisation, atavistic mobilisation based on the idea of the Other may not work as a mobilisation strategy.
3. Issues of language planning, shift and survival are integral to a contemporary and pro-active agenda of identity politics based on language.
4. An entire project, involving concerted efforts at the level of the government and complimented by similar private efforts is needed to prevent the declining use of Marathi language and promote its further development.
5. This would require comprehensive redesigning of the Marathi ideology in a manner that it takes cognisance of the contemporary internal and external challenges- local, national as well as global.

Methodology

This thesis is based on library research as well as data collection through interviews with open-ended questions. The research proposes to analyse the Samyukta Maharashtra Movement, Shivsena, Maharashtra Navnirman Sena and contemporary civil society movements focused on language issues. While doing this it draws upon the existing published material on these movements as well as interviews with some of the stakeholders and interpreting material not used by researchers so far.

Scheme of Chapters

Chapter I – Introduction

This chapter opens the topic for discussion. I begin by reviewing the literature on the subject. Some of the Studies of language politics deal with identity politics and within that ambit, look at language politics. Some are pan-Indian in approach. There are theoretical debates about the evolving nature of identity politics and its interface with the forces of globalisation. Together they give us an insight into the nature of language politics in India in general and Maharashtra in particular. Then there are studies dealing with the Samyukta Maharashtra Movement, Shivsena. Some of them are done by participants, whereas others by distant observers.

Lalji Pendse's diary of the Samyukta Maharashtra Movement deals with the dynamics of the movement. The author being a participant in the movement is passionate about it. He gives an insider's account of the movement for the creation of Unified Maharashtra. The book brings to the fore the Discourse of the Samyukta Maharashtra Movement. Dr Y.D. Phadke's thesis on the Samyukta Maharashtra Movement deals with politics of language in the aftermath of independence. It gives an elaborate analysis of the 'Samyukta Maharashtra Movement' on the backdrop of countrywide demands for linguistic reorganisation of states. Dr Phadke wrote eight volume history of Maharashtra (Visavya Shtakatil Maharashtra). Vol. 6-8 focus on the genesis and development of 'Samyukta Maharashtra Movement'. It gives huge resources for a researcher or an activist to compare and contrast the 'Samyukta Maharashtra Movement' with later political agencies like Shivsena and Maharashtra Navnirman Sena.

Mary Fainsod Katzenstein's 'Ethnicity and Equality: The Shiv Sena Party and Preferential Policies in Bombay' deals with the emergence of Shivsena against the backdrop of creation of unified Maharashtra. She deals with the techniques of mobilisation of urban middle class youth, the migration scenario and the response of the state that culminated into preferential policies. She discusses the issue of definition of Marathi that Shivsena espoused. This has repercussions for later developments in language politics in Maharashtra. Dipankar Gupta's book on Shivsena deals with the roots of Nativism and its impact on the politics of the state of Maharashtra. He rightly points out that the state Congress and the capitalist forces successfully used Shivsena to counter the threat of socialists and communists especially in the field of trade unions. He discusses Shivsena's use of violence as a strategy. Ironically, both these books do not discuss the roots of the Shivsena in the Samyukta Maharashtra Movement and the hopes that it created.

'Community Conflicts and the State in India, edited by Amruta Basu and Atul Kohli deals with the interface between conflict and regional / linguistic identities. It focuses on the crisis of governability intensified by identity. One of the articles written by Mary Fainsod Katzenstein, Uday Singh Mehta and Usha Thakkar titled 'The Rebirth of Shivsena, reviews Shivsena's conscious shift from the ideology of Sons-of-soil to Hindutva. It analyses contesting viewpoints about Shivsena's departure from nativist politics and causes thereof. It also focuses on the methods used by Shivsena to try and ensure the co-existence of the nativist and Hindutva agenda.

In addition to the books written by academicians, there are some written by journalists/ media persons. Vaibhav Purandare's 'Sena Story' is a journalistic account of the growth of Shivsena. Firsthand accounts of Shivsena leadership derived through interviews is strength of this book. The impressionistic nature of the account however makes it less useful for further studies. Prakash Akolkar's Marathi book on Shivsena (Jai Maharashtra) is more critical in nature and gives a detailed account of intra party politics within Shivsena and its drifting away from the Marathi agenda. It gives a detailed description of the pioneering work done by 'Sthaniya Lokadhikar Samiti' (Committee for the protection of the rights of locals).

"Maharashtratil Sattantar" by Rajendra Vora and Suhas Palshikar deals with the decline of the Congress and the rise of Shivsena – BJP alliance on the backdrop of 1995 Vidhansabha elections in Maharashtra through constituency and region-wise electoral statistics. It tries to establish the relationship between urbanisation, new economic policy and ascendancy of neo-fascist forces like Shivsena – BJP. In his edited volume 'Maharashtratil Sattasangharsha' (power struggle in Maharashtra), Dr Suhas Palshikar and his team give a statistical analysis of the performance of major political parties in Maharashtra. In his account of Shivsena, Palshikar asks few questions about the organisational structure of the Shivsena and its changing caste base. He deals with Shivsena's ideological discourse based on the appeal to masculinity as its core component. He suggests that violence, use of muscle power and encouraging resistance has been integral to the functioning of Shivsena. Palshikar argues that Shivsena's politics based on the opposition to the other is a product of inferiority complex of the Marathi speaking people. He does not see much benefit in Shivsena's exclusionist brand of politics. Thomas Blom Hansen's 'Urban violence in India: Identity politics, Mumbai and the postcolonial city' deals with the violence in the city of Mumbai especially the 1992-1993 riots and its impact on the identity of the city. In a way, it deals with 'Vernacularisation of democracy' in the country with special focus on the city. I present the analytical framework for the thesis in the next chapter.

Chapter II

This chapter provides the framework for the thesis. It begins with the discussion on constitutional provisions regarding language. These articles include provisions regarding cultural and educational rights, use of languages in the parliament and the state legislature, official language of the union, Provisions for increasing the use of Hindi, Regional languages, Languages of the Supreme Court and various High Courts and special directives regarding languages. This chapter also discusses the role played by the Department of Official Language under the Ministry of Home Affairs in the promotion of Hindi language. The Chapter also compares the institutionalised efforts for the promotion of Hindi language with the efforts taken by state governments for the promotion of regional languages. Together it provides for the constitutional framework within which I present language planning mechanisms for the development of Marathi.

Two concepts have to be juxtaposed with this constitutional framework. They are: Identity Politics and Globalisation. The term "identity politics" has come to signify a wide range of political activity and theorising founded in the shared experiences of injustice of members of certain social groups. What makes identity politics a significant departure from pre-identarian forms of the politics of recognition is its demand for recognition on the basis of the very grounds on which recognition has previously been denied. Critics argue that due to subjectivity, Identity Politics is prone to essentialism. Over a period of time, there is rapprochement between liberalism and identity politics. For many leftist commentators, identity politics is something of a bête noire, representing the capitulation to cultural criticism in place of analysis of the material roots of oppression. Marxists and socialists have often interpreted the perceived ascendancy of identity politics as representing the end of radical materialist critique. They argue that Identity politics is factionalising and depoliticising. It draws attention away from the ravages of late capitalism toward super structural cultural accommodations that leave economic structures unchanged.

Globalisation is variously defined in the literature on international relations and political science. Anthony Giddens describes it as the intensification of worldwide social relations which link distant localities in such a way that local happenings are shaped by events occurring many miles away and vice versa. Gilpin says that Globalisation is the integration of the world economy. It has also been described as time-space compression. Globalisation has been considered as a constitutive feature of the modern world. There are various types of globalisation: Political, Social, Economic and Cultural. Cultural Globalisation refers to the transmission of ideas, meanings and values across national borders. Through technological advancement, culture has been moving beyond borders and boundaries, transforming through locations the shared meanings of culture. Through the process of sharing, the ideas and values of one culture to another ultimately leads to interconnectedness between various populations from diverse cultures.

Language planning and development is a tool of empowerment of a language. Language planning is a deliberate effort to influence the function, structure, or acquisition of languages or language variety within a speech community. It is often associated with government planning, but also includes efforts of grass-roots organisations and even individuals. Linguistic rights (or language rights or linguistic human rights) are the human and civil rights concerning the individual and collective right to choose the language or languages for communication in a private or public atmosphere. Linguistic rights include, among others, the right to one's own language in legal, administrative and judicial acts, language education, and media in a language understood and freely chosen by those concerned.

Many countries have a language policy designed to favour or discourage the use of a particular language or set of languages. Although nations historically have used language policies most often to promote one official language at the expense of others, many countries now have policies designed to protect and promote regional and ethnic languages. Language policy is what a government does either officially through legislation, court decisions or policy to determine how languages are used, to cultivate language skills needed to meet national priorities or to establish the rights of individuals or groups to use and maintain languages.

Thus, the chapter creates a suitable framework to understand the constitutional design on languages and specific efforts to develop a particular language through meticulous planning. It is to the evolution of the Marathi consciousness through the Samyukta Maharashtra Movement that we move next.

Chapter III

Samyukta Maharashtra Movement

This chapter deals with the evolution of the Marathi language and Maharashtra since the Satavahan Period. It analyses the various stages in this evolution. Then it focuses on the demand for Unified Maharashtra emerged during the freedom movement, the response to this demand from the Congress High Command, the emergence of a non-Congress Coalition in the form of Samyukta Maharashtra Samiti and the various challenges encountered in the process.

The British divided India into administrative provinces. There was no concern for the history, culture or nationality of the Indians. Before independence, a number of linguistic communities were demanding for homogenous regions. Although the principle of linguistic reorganisation of states was accepted, the actual process of redrawing boundaries of states was not smooth.

The demand for the creation of Unified Maharashtra dates back to the late nineteenth century. However, support for this demand was consolidated in the twentieth century. There were many hurdles in the creation of Unified Maharashtra. They are listed below:

- The inclusion of the city of Bombay in Maharashtra.
- The dissolution of Nizam's Hyderabad and the inclusion of Marathi speaking areas of Marathwada in Maharashtra.

- Negotiations with the leadership of Vidarbha so that some of them demanding for Separate Mahavidarbha state give up that demand and join Maharashtra.
- Inclusion of Goa in Maharashtra after its liberation, since Konkani is a dialect of Marathi.
- Inclusion of the border areas of Belgaon, Karwar and Nipani in Maharashtra by settling the dispute with the state of Mysore.
- Including the Dangs district bordering Gujarat in Maharashtra, since Dangi was a dialect of Marathi.

Dar Commission Report stated that the demand for linguistic states is parochial, regressive and regionalistic in nature. It would lead to large scale migration of population and bloodshed. It would lead to the breakup of the country, because at the root of the demand for linguistic reorganisation of states is the idea of sub-nationalism.' While criticising the demand for Unified Maharashtra, the report said that Maharashtrians are aggressive and feudal in mindset. Maharashtra has no right over Mumbai. It can't be included in one region because it belongs to the entire country. There was outrage in Maharashtra over the decision of the commission and its observations about Maharashtra.

A new Committee consisting of Jawaharlal Nehru, Vallabhbhai Patel and Pattabhi Sitaramayya (popularly called JVP Committee) opined that the atmosphere in the country was not conducive for reorganisation of states. However, Congress being committed to linguistic reorganisation of States, stated that the plan will be supported provided it doesn't harm the defense, unity and economic prosperity of the country. About Mumbai the report said that the suggestion that it is dominated by one language and therefore should be included in a unilingual state can't even be considered. The committee recommended that Maharashtra should be eventually carved excluding the city of Bombay.

After the creation of Unilingual Andhra Pradesh, a commission headed by Fazal Ali and consisting of members like Sardar Panikkar and H.N. Kunzru (popularly called as States Reorganisation Commission or SRC) was appointed in 1953 to recommend the redrawing of boundaries on linguistic basis. As far as Maharashtra was concerned, the SRC report rejected the demand of Unified Maharashtra with the inclusion of city of Bombay. It recommended the creation of Vidarbha state. The Marathi speaking areas of Belgaon district were given to the Mysore state. A bilingual Bombay state consisting of the Marathi and Gujarati speaking areas was created. On 16th January 1956, Nehru announced that Bombay would be made a Union Territory, Maharashtra would be created with the inclusion of Vidarbha and Gujarat would be created with the inclusion of Saurashtra and Kutch. This was in complete violation of the principles of state reorganisation and more importantly, against the wishes of the people of Maharashtra. While the future of Maharashtra with the inclusion of the city of Bombay was still uncertain, leaders from different regions of the state had come together to decide the arrangement after the creation of Maharashtra. They signed the Nagpur Pact.

Eleven parties were the constituents of the Samyukta Maharashtra Samiti. The objectives of the Samyukta Maharashtra Samiti were as follows:

(a) Creation of unified Maharashtra as per the principles of the linguistic reorganisation of states.

(b) Establishment of the principles of democracy and socialism in Maharashtra and executing the programmes of the Samiti.

(c) Developing the economic, social and cultural life of Maharashtra on socialistic principles.

Shankarrao Deo first talked about bringing the 'Mangal Kalash' of Samyukta Maharashtra. However, he was not successful in doing that. Ironically, Yashwantrao Chavan got the opportunity to bring the 'Mangal Kalash' of Maharashtra. The Central Government had planned two states that is Bombay and Gujarat. However, the leaders of the Samiti insisted on the name Maharashtra and very reluctantly the Congress high command accepted this demand.

The struggle for unified Maharashtra was not exclusionist in nature. The idea was not to demand Maharashtra for Maharashtrians only. Protection of education, cultural movements and civil rights of non-Maharashtrians was properly taken care of. All parties and their leaders took utmost care to ensure that the movement doesn't lead to hatred towards a linguistic community. After the creation of unified Maharashtra, the Samyukta Maharashtra Samiti was split and was renamed Sampoorna Maharashtra Samiti.

Chapter IV

Congress and Language Politics in Maharashtra

This chapter analyses the role played by the Congress Party in the promotion of Marathi language after the creation of Maharashtra. It also deals with systemic failures and various trends of language politics in the Congress era.

It was the fear of losing the 1962 Lok Sabha and Vidhan Sabha elections that had prompted the Congress High Command to take immediate positive steps about the creation of Samyukta Maharashtra. Yashwantrao Chavan, the Chief Minister of the bilingual Bombay state, tried to convince Indira Gandhi, the then President of the Congress party, who in turn convinced Jawaharlal Nehru. During the Samyukta Maharashtra Movement, Chavan was severely criticised by the leaders of the Movement for his allegiance to Nehru and refusal to accept that the Marathi speaking people were really unhappy with the experiment of the Bigger Bilingual state of which Chavan was the Chief Minister. Chavan's successful negotiation with the Congress High Command for granting statehood and the grand ceremony of the creation of Unified Maharashtra helped him regain the affection of the people of Maharashtra. Thus, onwards he worked very hard to rebuild his image as the spokesperson of Marathi language and culture.

Immediately after the creation of the state, Chavan established the following language, literature and culture related bodies.

- Bhasha Sanchalanalay (Directorate of languages).

- Sahitya ani Sanskruti Mandal (board for literature and culture).
- Vishwakosh Nirmiti Mandal (Board for Marathi Encyclopedia).
- Vidyapeeth Grantha Nirmiti Mandal (Board for creation of university level reference books).

From the beginning, no thought was given to the autonomy of these institutions. Therefore, they remained under the tighter control of the bureaucracy, which was generally ignorant or indifferent to the promotion of Marathi. The Maharashtra Official Languages Act 1964 was passed in 1965. A language advisory committee was established to aid and advice the government about the enhanced use of Marathi in the administration.

The Directorate of Language has published two booklets-Compilations of rules and orders issued by the Government of Maharashtra for the effective implementation of the Maharashtra Official Languages Act 1964. The first volume includes rules and orders issued from 1965 to December 1987 and the supplementary volume includes rules and orders from January 1988 to July 1993. The orders are related to four issues. Majority of the government orders are about increasing the use of Marathi in the functioning of the State Government. The tone and tenor of these circulars keeps on changing depending on the need of the government and compliance or non-compliance of government departments. Most of the circulars are issued by the desk in the Directorate of Languages looking after increasing the use of Marathi in state administration. Nowhere had the government set any deadline for complete shift to Marathi after which the defaulted employees would be penalised. Shivsena either did not understand the issue of use of Marathi in administration or did not find it important to act upon. The linguistic composition of the senior bureaucracy did play a negative role in the implementation of language policy.

Very few literary figures understand that the development of language in different domains of social life is a specialised task and has to be dealt by linguists. Not all in the literary fraternity appreciate that they have to be proactive in the development of the language.

At the all-India level there were growing concerns about the use of regional languages in administration for transparency and accountability besides ensuring enhanced participation of the masses in administration. In order to address these pressing issues, the year 1979 was declared as Raj Bhasha Varsha (Official Languages Year). It was an attempt to boost the confidence of those who propagated an enhanced role for regional languages in administration.

One of the objectives of the initial language policy of the Government of Maharashtra was to make Marathi the language of higher knowledge in all the disciplines of modern life and ensure that it becomes the medium of instruction at the graduate and post graduate level. To this end, Vidyapeeth Grantha Nirmiti Mandal was established. The objective was to create university level texts so that students and teachers get adequate reference material when Marathi becomes the medium of instruction at the graduate and post graduate level. Clause 5 (55) of the Maharashtra Universities Act 1994 says that it is part of the power and duties of the University to promote by itself, or in cooperation with other Universities the study of Marathi and the use of Marathi as a medium of instruction, study, research and examination. However, soon Universities started dragging their feet on setting up a deadline for making Marathi available as the medium of instruction. As the gap between English and Marathi medium widened and almost became unbridgeable, the position of the universities became more and more ambivalent. Around 20 years back, Vidyapeeth Grantha Nirmiti Mandal was closed down arbitrarily.

A close overview of the functioning of Maharashtra Government's language and literary agencies gives us the feeling that the state is at best inefficient and at worst indifferent towards language related issues. The state government has paid notional tribute to its official language. Within the Congress leadership also there seems to be a difference in approach. Those with grassroot support and mass following like Yashwantrao Chavan, Vasantdada Patil, and Sharad Pawar have taken initiative in the development of Marathi.

Since the time of the Samyukta Maharashtra Movement, the Congress leadership has been apologetic about expressing concerns about Marathi language and Marathi Manoos. They are generally worried that the non-Marathi higher leadership of the Congress would consider it parochial, regressive and that may affect their prospects of upward mobility within the party. Strangely, this guilt sense is prevalent mainly among the Congressmen among Maharashtra. Congressmen from other regions take up issues of their regional languages.

It is true that merely state initiative doesn't entirely contribute to the development of a language. It has to be ably supported by various stakeholders like schools and universities, libraries, literary and linguistic organisations, language activists, political parties etc. One has to keep in mind that the efforts of promotion of a language would reach a dead-end if a language can't help people in earning livelihood. Therefore, empowerment of language and empowerment of a linguistic community are closely related to each other.

Chapter V

Shivsena and other political parties in the opposition and language politics in Maharashtra

This chapter deals with the role played by political parties like Shivsena, BJP and Maharashtra Navnirman Sena in furthering the cause of Marathi. The declining importance of Maharashtrians in the political economy of the city of Mumbai was a matter of serious concern much before the arrival of Shivsena. Maharashtrians were the single largest community in Mumbai. However, the economic power was still in the hands of non-Marathis. Shivsena's initial targets were South Indians, especially Tamilian and Malayalese, who they thought were taking away the clerical and officer level jobs from Maharashtrians. When Bal Thackeray decided to establish

Shivsena, he put forward a list of duties for the Marathi Manoos and expectations from the Government of Maharashtra. One thing is clear that for the Shivsena, the point of agony was not the condition of the Marathi language but the declining condition of the urban middle and lower middle class Marathi youth situated in metropolitan cities like Mumbai. Thus, the Shivsena, began its career with ventilating the grievances of the Marathi Manoos about employment and not by talking about about the decline of the Marathi language. Eventually, Shivsena did take up the issue of Marathi language, but in the strictest sense of the term, it was not playing the politics of language. It was the politics of perceived or real injustice against a linguistic community.

The understanding of Shivsena about the problem of Marathi was based on the spontaneous response of people. It seems that Thackeray never had any comprehensive ideology in mind. The anti-component of the ideology was very strong. They were anti-South Indians, anti-Communist and anti-Muslims. Besides the issue of employment to Marathi youth, Shivsena has undertaken various activities through which it tried to mobilise the Marathi Manoos and become a political force to reckon with. It established various allied wings. Out of all these organisations, Sthaniy Lokadhikar Samiti and later on Sthaniy Lokadhikar Samiti Mahasangh has played a key role in awareness about employment opportunities.

The 1980's saw a shift in Shivsena ideology from Marathi Manoos to Hindu Jan. Post-1999, Thackeray prepared room for Uddhav and Raj. Raj revolted against Uddhav's dominance. In course of time, Raj Thackeray established Maharashtra Navnirman Sena [MNS]. The expulsion of Narayan Rane and the establishment of a new party by Raj Thackeray created a crisis of credibility and existence for the Shivsena.

Shivsena was able to enter the interiors of Maharashtra with the help of Hindutva ideology. As stated earlier, this had less to do with the limitations of the Marathi ideology and more to do with the inability of Shivsena to comprehend the complexities of Marathi agenda in general. When Shivsena officially shifted to Hindutva for electoral benefits, it had to accommodate all non-Maharashtrians because of the ideological demands. In such cases, the more encompassing ideology silently kills the less encompassing ideology. This is a fundamental problem in combining the Marathi ideology with Hindutva. Shivsena therefore has neither been truly Hindu nor truly Maharashtrian post-1985. The fact that Shivsena still monopolised the Marathi tag reveals that no parallel organisation emerged that could expose the limitations of Shivsena for a more comprehensive ideology. The support from youth and educated strata are two major features of Shivsena's support base. The success of Shivsena lies in following a non-conformist technique of militant politics. Post-1980, this spontaneous militancy was replaced by routinisation and bureaucratisation. The problem that Shivsena faces is not unique. Movements like DMK or Assam Gana Parishad have gone through a similar process.

MNS was established in 2006 by Raj Thackeray. The flag of his party includes the green and the blue colour. This has been interpreted as his party's openness towards Dalits and Muslims. The MNS is anti-migrants like the Shivsena. The difference lies in the target of aggression. MNS believes that the North Indian influx is part of a political design. The definition of Marathi Manoos is different in the case of both the parties. Shivsena defined Marathi Manoos as someone whose mother tongue is Marathi. Later, developments forced the Shivsena to adopt a more accommodative definition whereby Marathi as the Mother tongue did not remain a defining criterion. Like the Shivsena, even MNS does not want to exclusively focus on street action or peaceful agitation. MNS makes no distinction between constructive and conflicting ways and believes that both go hand in hand. Thus, street agitations marked by violence are an important and authentic feature of the MNS. After the arrival of MNS on the political front, both MNS and Shivsena had to confront certain issues. Interestingly there was a role reversal in their campaigns.

Besides the Sena and MNS, other political parties in Maharashtra include left of the centre political parties like The socialist Parties (PSP and SSP), Communist Parties (CPI and CPM), Peasants and Workers Party; Right of the centre parties like Jan Sangh and BJP, and various factions of the RPI. The PSP and the CPI were part of the Samyukta Maharashtra Movement. However, they differed on the issue of continuation of the struggle after the creation of Maharashtra. Then onwards, except during the days of the PDF government, socialists and communists have never shared power. Jan Sangh was in power during the PDF government from 1978-1980. After 1985 the BJP joined hands with the Shivsena. Therefore, although it did not directly talk about the issues of Marathi Language, it did share the concerns raised by Shivsena as an alliance partner. The Scheduled Caste Federation of Babasaheb Ambedkar had participated in the Samyukta Maharashtra Movement. However, after Ambedkar's death various factions of the RPI have not discussed issues of language in detail. Most of the times factions of the RPI are lesser important partners of the electoral alliance and their leaders are co-opted by major political parties. That could be one reason why these parties have not discussed such issues in great detail. The PWP was also a member of the Samyukta Maharashtra Movement. After the creation of Maharashtra, many Maratha leaders of the party went to the Congress responding to the appeal of Yashwantrao Chavan. Like the Socialist and the Communist parties even the influence of PWP is restricted to few pockets in the state. It would be difficult to expect much from political parties on the margins of political life in Maharashtra to take up language issues beyond their strength in the legislature.

Chapter VI

Civil Society Movements and language politics in Maharashtra

Political parties are not the only agencies that look after the issues of Marathi language and culture. There are civil society organisations working on these issues since the creation of the state. The idea of Civil Society is not new in the discussion on politics. Civil Society Organisations (CSOs) refer to a wide array of organisations: community groups, non-governmental organisations (NGOs), labour unions, indigenous groups, charitable organisations, faith-based organisations, professional associations, and foundations".

Maharashtra has a strong presence of civil society organisations. They work in various domains like education, health, gender justice, Dalit or tribal rights. There are not many in the domain of language and culture. Civil society organisations have an option to join a political party and carry their agenda forward. However, that may compromise their autonomy. More importantly, the perspective of mainstream political parties working for Marathi language and the approach of many civil society organisations is not similar. More so, civil society organisations do not have a common platform to strengthen themselves and avoid duplication of work. Thus, civil society organisations are caught between the devil and the deep sea. Efforts have been made by Marathi Abhyas Kendra and Marathi Ekjoot to bring together civil society activists working for Marathi language. However, these efforts have not borne fruit.

Chapter VII

The politics of Marathi in times of Globalisation

One has to understand the limitations of the multiple existing versions of language politics in Maharashtra. Critique of the present versions of language politics can be summarised as below:

1. It is anti-national because it challenges the constitutional principle of mobility of people across the country.
2. It is violent and street driven weaker sections of the society are hit hard by hooliganism.
3. It is undemocratic because the parties that champion the cause of Marathi language follow an authoritarian party structure.
4. It is fascist in nature because they silence the critics using muscle power and therefore no meaningful debate is possible to evaluate the agenda.

5. It regressive and backward looking because it goes against contemporary global trends.
6. It is symbolic and reactionary because language is used for electoral gains.
7. It is hegemonic in nature because its proponents propagate the language of the elites or upper castes and upper classes. Language becomes a disguised weapon for those who want to push caste exploitation under the carpet through summary use of emotive language issues.
8. Language is not a core issue but only a symptom of more urgent problems. Focusing on language issues amounts to alteration of priorities.

Civil society organisations working on Marathi language and culture have been criticised for their piecemeal approach, lack of organisational abilities and lack of ability to impact the political system. The most relevant and poignant question: Is it possible to develop the agenda of Marathi language, culture and Marathi Manoos in a manner that has not been done so far? Secondly, what would be the ideological framework of such a movement? We need to chalk out some way whereby this dichotomy between loyalty to the Indian nation-state and genuine expression of linguistic interests of its people is addressed. Proactive preservation of the Maharashtrian identity along with connectedness with the Indian identity could be a possible solution.

- No effort of alternate language politics is possible in Maharashtra without satisfactorily addressing nationalism and globalisation. Language is essentially a political issue and therefore it has to be suitably handled through a language based political movement. Such a movement has to develop an innovative and durable linkage between Marathi language, culture and economic interests of the Marathi speaking people.

Unless language development is combined with a comprehensive understanding of development of a linguistic community, it is not going to succeed. Once the ideology is put in place we can move on to the plan of action. It will include the following:

- *language policy* for the state.
- the restructuring of the Centre-State relations.
- developing institutional mechanisms for the development of languages and making available adequate infrastructure.
- Language planning for the development of Marathi language.
- Comprehensive use of Marathi in the Administration of Maharashtra.
- programme for enhancing the use of Marathi in all strata of judiciary.
- use of Marathi in information and communication technology.
- empower Marathi Arthakaran.
- expand the scope of Marathi education.

Conclusion

Looking at the stalemate in the present form of language politics in Maharashtra, it is imperative to look at the linkage between language, culture and the economic and political interests of a linguistic community in an innovative way. It is through a comprehensive ideology and a detailed plan of action that this ambitious task can be accomplished.

Bibliography

Official Resource

- Department of official language, Ministry of Home Affairs, Government of India http://rajbhasha.nic.in/
- Websites of Language agencies of Government of Maharashtra.

Sahitya Sanskruti Mandal (Board for Development of Literature and Culture)

http://mahasahityasanskriti.maharashtra.gov.in/index.htm

Rajya Marathi Vikas Sanstha (State Institute for the Development of Marathi)

http://rmvs.maharashtra.gov.in/rmvs/?q=home

Bhasha Sanchalanalay (Directorate of language) http://www.gms.maharashtra.gov.in/bhasha/PrashasanikLekhanKosh.aspx

Vishvakosh Nirmiti Mandal (Board for production of Marathi Encyclopedia)

http://www.vishwakosh.org.in/vis/

Website of Maharashtra Navnirman Sena (MNS) www.manase.org

Manifestoes of

1. Indian National Congress
2. Nationalist Congress Party
3. Shivsena
4. Bharatiya Janasangha
5. Bharatiya Janata Party
6. Communist Party of India (CPI)
7. Communist Party of India – Marxist CPI(M)
8. Peasants and Workers' Party
9. Maharashtra Navnirman Sena

A compilation of Maharashtra Official Language Act 1964 and rules, orders issued therein -Bhasha Sanchalanalay (Directorate of Languages), Mumbai, 1988

Websites

- http://plato.stanford.edu/
- http://bitbucket.icaap.org/ Online dictionary of social sciences

Journals, periodicals and Yearbooks

- Seminar
- Sadhana
- Economic and Political Weekly
- Samaj Prabodhan Patrika
- Anubhav
- Navbharat
- Bhasha Ani Jeevan
- Ruchi
- The Marxist
- Kalnirnay Sanskrutik

Books

- Akolkar, Prakash, Jai Maharashtra, Ha Shivsena Navacha Itihas ahe (Mumbai, Prabhat Prakashan, 1998).
- Anderson, Benedict, Imagined Communities: Reflections on the Origin and Spread of Nationalism. (Revised Edition ed. London and New York: Verso, 1991, pp. 5-7).
- Basu, Amruta and Kohli Atul (Ed.) Community Conflicts and the State in India – (OUP, 1998).
- Bipin Chandra, Mridula Mukherjee and Aditya Mukherjee (ed.), India after Independence 1947-2000 (2000, Penguin books).
- Bourdieu, Pierre, The Logic of Practice, (Stanford University Press, Stanford California 1990) p. 56.
- Brass, Paul, Ethnicity and Nationalism, Theory and Comparison, (Sage publications, 1991) p.18.
- Downing, John; Ali Mohammadi, Annabelle Sreberny-Mohammadi (1995), Questioning the media: a critical introduction (2, illustrated Ed.). SAGE, p. 482.
- Dr Suhas Palshikar (Ed.), Maharashtratil Sattasangharsha' (Samakalin Prakashan, Pune, 2007).

- Ghosh, Partha S., Ethnicity versus Nationalism – The Devolution discourse in Sri Lanka, Phillipson, Robert - Linguistic Imperialism, 1992 and Linguistic imperialism continued (Orient Black Swan, 2009).
- Giddens, Anthony, The Consequences of Modernity. (Cambridge: Polity,1990).
- Gilpin, Robert, Global Political Economy: Understanding the International Economic Order (Princeton University Press, 2001).
- Gupta, Dipankar, Nativism in a metropolis: Shivsena in Bombay, (Mumbai, Manohar, 1982.
- Gupta, Jyotirindra Das, Language Conflict and National Development: Group Politics and National Language Policy in India. (University of California Press, 1970).
- Hansen, Thomas Blom, Urban violence in India: Identity politics, Mumbai and the postcolonial city, (Permanent black, 2001).
- Joshi, Manohar, Shivsena, Kaal, Aaj, Udya - History of Shivsena from 1966, (Mumbai, Prabodhan Prakashan, 2008.
- Katzenstein, Mary Fainsod, Ethnicity and Equality: The Shiv Sena Party and Preferential Policies in Bombay (Cornell University Press, l979).
- Kymlicka, Will, Multicultural Citizenship: A Liberal Theory of Minority Rights (Oxford: Oxford University Press, 1995).
- Lee, Siu-Nam Lee (1988), "Communication imperialism and dependency: A conceptual clarification." International Communication Gazette (Netherlands: Kiuwer Academic Publishers) (41): 74.
- McPhail, Thomas L. (1987), Electronic colonialism: the future of international broadcasting and communication. Volume 126 of Sage library of social research. Sage Publications, p. 18.

- Nahir, Moshe-Language Planning Goals: A classification. (First published in 1984). Republished in Christina B. Paulston and Richard Tucker, eds., Sociolinguistics: The Essential Readings, pp. 423-448. (Oxford: Blackwell, 2003).
- Parekh, Bhikhu, Rethinking Multiculturalism: Cultural Diversity and Political Theory. (Harvard, UP, 2002).
- Pendse, Lalji- Maharashtrache Mahamanthan, 2nd edition, (Mumbai, Lokwangmay Griha, May 2010).
- Phadke, Dr Y.D., Politics and language: (Mumbai Himalaya Publishing House).
- Phillipson, Robert, Linguistic Imperialism (Oxford University Press, 1992).
- Purandare, Vaibhav, The Sena Story –(Mumbai Business Publications Inc, 1999).
- Rahman, Tariq, Language and politics in Pakistan: (Orient Longman, 2007).
- Rahman, Tariq, Language Ideology and power – Language learning among the Muslims of Pakistan and North India, (Orient Longman, 2000).
- Robert, D King, Nehru and the Language Politics of India (1997, OUP).
- Sahasrabuddhe, P.G., Maharashtra Sanskruti, 4th edition (Continental Prakashan, Pune, 2011).
- Scholte, Jan Aart, Globalisation: A Critical Introduction (London Macmillan 2000).
- Smith, Anthony D, The Ethnic Origins of Nations. (Blackwell, 1987).
- Varshney, Ashutosh, Ethnic Conflict and Civic Life: Hindus and Muslims in India (Yale University Press, 2002 and 2003).
- Vora, Rajendra, Palshikar Suhas, Maharashtratil Sattantar (Granthali, Mumbai, 1996).

Index